# MAKING
# YOUR VISION
# A REALITY

## OTHER FORTHCOMING PARKER BOOKS

*African-American Church Leadership,* edited by Lee N. June
*Elijah's Mantle,* edited by Diane Proctor Reeder

PARKER BOOKS

# MAKING YOUR VISION A REALITY

## Proven Steps to Develop and Implement Your Church Vision Plan

## Paul Cannings, PhD

Kregel
*Ministry*

*Making Your Vision a Reality: Proven Steps to Develop and Implement Your Church Vision Plan*

Published by Kregel Publications, a division of Kregel, Inc., P.O. Box 2607, Grand Rapids, MI 49501.

Parker Books was conceived by Matthew Parker, the president of the Institute for Black Family Development, Detroit, MI, and is an imprint that provides books for Christian ministry leaders.

Please send your comments and requests for information about Power Walk Ministries or Living Word Fellowship Church to the address below:

Power Walk Ministries/Living Word Fellowship Church
7350 TC Jester
Houston, TX 77088
Telephone: (281) 260–7402
www.powerwalkministries.org
www.lwfellowshipchurch.org/

**Library of Congress Cataloging-in-Publication Data**
Cannings, Paul, 1957–
    Making your vision a reality : proven steps to develop and implement your church vision plan / Paul Cannings.
        p. cm.
    1. Church growth. 2. Christian leadership. 3. Pastoral theology. 4. Church management. I. Title.
        BV652.25.C36 2012
        254—dc23

                                                                                2012035554

ISBN 978-0-8254-4274-2

*Printed in the United States of America*
13  14  15  16  17 / 5  4  3  2  1

# CONTENTS

Introduction .................................................................. 7

Chapter 1:  The Need for Vision ................................... 13

Chapter 2:  A Biblical Overview of
            the New Testament Church ......................... 21

Chapter 3:  Designing Your Church's Vision ................... 33

Chapter 4:  Proceeding from Vision to
            Strategy Development ................................ 41

Chapter 5:  Moving from Vision to Ministry ................... 51

Chapter 6:  Leadership That Makes a Difference ............ 85

Chapter 7:  Selecting Leaders to Shape the Vision ......... 95

Chapter 8:  Staffing the Strategy ................................ 109

Chapter 9:  Designing a Budget
            That Empowers the Vision ......................... 145

Chapter 10: Conclusion .............................................. 153

Appendix:  Ministry Flow Charts ................................ 157

# INTRODUCTION

Over the years, I have had the privilege of working with pastors and leaders nationally and internationally. I have yet to meet a pastor who did not have some idea of what he wanted to see happen in the church God placed in his care. Some ideas were for the short term and others were long-term plans. There was one common thread however; they had a hard time crafting a vision and executing a sound plan in cooperation with their chosen leaders. They had no problems executing short-term plans, such as completing building programs or buying vans. But those plans only created a need for more and more plans, leading to unnecessary pressure and stress. The result is an endless repetition of short-term plans with no overarching mission or vision. Wandering from program to program. Sunday-to-Sunday "drift." Ultimately, it is the parishioners who suffer.

It is not that some of these pastors did not have a passion for the Gospel and discipleship; they just don't know how to craft and implement a vision. The struggles are many and particular to each congregation, including lack of support from the elder or deacon boards, challenges from outspoken parishioners, unhealthy nostalgia for past, man-made traditions. The pastor is then faced with going from Sunday to Sunday with no clear idea of a vision or how to effectively lead.

Some pastors, for the sake of their families, decide to focus on preaching, teaching, counseling, caring for the sick…and praying for church growth. But this latter topic—church growth—needs both prayer and action. The resultant questions are inevitable. Where are we going? Why are people leaving? Why is there no clear direction for the church? All of these questions end up on the doorstep of the pastor. Many pastors become disillusioned and begin looking for greener pastures. The members then become disillusioned even as they wonder why pastors are not staying long, but they do little to help turn things around.

## MOSES: GOD'S EXAMPLE FOR LEADERS

There was no question that Moses was God's called leader. God presented this visibly to the people on a daily basis (Exod. 33:7–12). There was no debate on what they were supposed to do and where they needed to go. They understood that they left Egypt to enter the land that was promised for over 400 years. Moses then sent out spies to the Promised Land (Num. 13). These spies were courageous enough to go throughout the land that God had prepared for them. They were committed. They stayed until they had a good understanding of what was in the land. Unfortunately, 10 out of 12 of them shrunk back from entering the land because of fear.

> Then Caleb silenced the people before Moses and said, "We should go up and take possession of the land, for we can certainly do it." But the men who had gone up with him said, "We can't attack those people; they are stronger than we are." And they spread among the Israelites a bad report about the land they had explored. They said, "The land we explored devours those living in it. All the people we saw there are of great size. We saw the Nephilim there (the descendants of Anak come from the Nephilim). We seemed like grasshoppers in our own eyes, and we looked the same to them" (Num. 13:30–33).

When they saw difficulties ahead, these leaders persuaded the people to follow them rather than Moses and as a result the people perished for a lack of vision (Prov. 29:18). The people wandered for 40 years without a vision, therefore without meaning. A whole group of people died because leaders refused to follow God's vision that was presented through His chosen leader.

Many, if not all believers, would agree that Christ died for the church and it is His shed blood that allows us all to be in His kingdom. Most believers would agree that Christ is the head of the church (Col. 1:18) and the church is designed to be a structure that represents Christ's body on earth (Eph.. 1:22–23; 1 Cor. 12:4–7, 27). Most members of the church and its leaders would agree that God calls a pastor into ministry (Eph. 4:11). But while they give assent to these principles, they have a hard time applying them to their roles within their own churches.

This book is designed to address these issues because it is only through the church that Christ accomplishes His plan to all mankind. "And He put all things in subjection under His feet, and gave Him as head over all things to the church" (Eph. 1:22). Paul goes on to inform us that this is done "In order that the manifold wisdom of God might now be made known through the church to the rulers and authorities in heavenly places" (Eph. 3:10). It is only through the church that Satan's gates can be locked or opened (Matt. 16:18–19).

Please understand that as far as God is concerned, He has provided the plan.

> He made known to us the mystery of His will, according to His kind intention which He purposed in Him with a view to an administration suitable to the fullness of the times, that is, the summing up of all things in Christ, things in the heavens and things on the earth. In Him also we have obtained an inheritance, having been predestined according to His purpose who works all things after the counsel of His will, to the end that we who were the first to hope in Christ would be to the praise of His glory (Eph. 1:9–12).

Christ has also provided all the ministries of the Church, His body and the Helper, the Holy Spirit to accomplish the plan (1 Cor. 12:4–7). This is why it is of extreme importance that we address how leaders in the church lead and at the same time work with the pastor to develop a vision for the church. This allows for the pastor to exercise his appropriate leadership role.

Many churches have died, or gone to sleep spiritually. They struggle with church growth as they go from one Sunday to the next. No one is being baptized; no souls are being won. Bible study attendance is low and worship continues with the same songs and the same order of worship "that was sent from heaven" before the pastor came. This book will try to address these issues so that there is accountability not just for the pastor but also for the leaders, with the ultimate goal that God's plans are accomplished and His people do not perish.

> According to the grace of God which was given to me, like a wise master builder I laid a foundation, and another is building on it. But each man must be careful how he builds on it. For no man can lay a foundation other

than the one which is laid, which is Jesus Christ. Now if any man builds on the foundation with gold, silver, precious stones, wood, hay, straw, each man's work will become evident; for the day will show it because it is to be revealed with fire, and the fire itself will test the quality of each man's work. If any man's work, which he has built on it remains, he will receive a reward. If any man's work is burned up, he will suffer loss; but he himself will be saved, yet so as through fire (1 Cor. 3:10–15).

There are only few leaders who do not have a passion to see their church mature to impact the lives of believers. We can look to the Judges story of Deborah and Barak as an example. Deborah was not called by God to lead the people; Barak was the one who God in His sovereign will called. Deborah understood her role as a civil judge and sat under a palm tree between Ramah and Bethel each day. Being a prophetess, she understood that God would speak to her about His calling of Barak (Jud. 4:6). Being in a war against a rootless oppressor, the wife of Lappidoth was not called for this task.

However, while the oppression of the Hebrews continued, Barak functioned as always (Jud. 4:3). The severe oppression went on for 20 years. When Barak finally responded, he said he would lead only if Deborah would come with him. "If you will go with me, then I will go; but if you will not go with me, I will not go" (Jud. 4:8.)

Maybe Barak needed her because he knew God spoke to her and she was a woman led by God and respected by the people. Maybe Barak was intimidated because these people inflected severe punishment on Israel for twenty years. I don't know. I do know one thing though, Barak was not a leader. He had no initiative to do anything about the oppression, and he lacked the courage to do what God instructed him to do. It is like what I heard one of my boys say to the other one night when the second floor of our house was left dark: "If you go to the top of the stairs, then I'll come upstairs with you." A pastor may not take the initiative to lead the church, but that does not mean that the leaders must lead for him. The leaders must work with the pastor to stimulate or hold him up in his called position. That is what Deborah did for Barak.

This is a process I will address in this book because God does not adjust His structure, no matter how strong the other leaders are compared to the pastor. Notice, even though Deborah went out to war with Barak, God honored Barak in Hebrews 11:32 because he did obey God (whether it was the ideal way or not) and risked his life to defend his country. The question is, how can a leader go from great ideas to a productive process, which is implemented in such a manner that it forms a strategy that defines the nature and function of the church? The process is critical: it must define everything about the church and its function in a structure that can be measured.

This is a nuts-and-bolts book that outlines a systematic process that will help shape your church's vision statement. That process will include designing strategies for implementation of the vision; outlining the role of leadership and the role of members; and showing how the vision shapes the church budget. The goal is to provide church pastors and leaders with a mechanism for establishing a clear vision and direction. I have worked with many churches to help them in this process, and this book is a compilation of the best practices from all of those assignments. This book is a resource that can guide any church through the critical development and implementation of its vision.

## Chapter One

# THE NEED FOR VISION

W"here there is no vision, the people are unrestrained, but happy is he who keeps the law" (Prov. 29:18). The meaning of the word "vision" is a divine message heard by a prophet. A vision is no good if the person outlining the vision does not have a heart for God's Word as the authority for their lives. God calls pastors/teachers whose job it is to give wisdom and knowledge (Jer. 3:15) and to equip believers so that by their works of service they grow up to "attain to the unity of the faith, and of the knowledge of the Son of God, to a mature man, to the measure of the stature which belongs to the fullness of Christ" (Eph. 4:12–13). This knowledge is attained through the diligent study of God's Word (2 Tim. 2:15), which provides all the information necessary to do the work of God (2 Tim. 3:14–17).

> All Scripture is inspired by God and profitable for teaching, for reproof, for correction, for training in righteousness; *so that the man of God may be adequate, equipped for every good work* (2 Tim. 3:16–17; emphasis mine).

It is from this knowledge that the Holy Spirit inspires the work of the pastor and transforms the life of a believer (1 Tim. 4:11–16; 2 Tim. 4:1–8; Rom. 12:2; Col. 1:9–11) so that the will of God moves from a knowledge base to a daily development of the kingdom of God constantly being manifested upon the earth (Luke 17:21).

Believers live productive lives because the Word of God serves as a comprehensive source for their daily needs.

> Grace and peace be multiplied to you in the knowledge of God and of Jesus our Lord; seeing that His divine power has granted to us everything pertaining to life and godliness, through the true knowledge of Him who called us by His own glory and excellence. For by these He has granted to us His precious and magnificent promises, so that by them you may become partakers of the divine nature, having escaped the corruption that is in the world by lust (2 Pet. 1:2–4).

The vision that a pastor develops must come from the very sources that equips him for every good work (2 Tim. 3:16) as he equips believers to do work of services (Eph. 4:12), from the very source that empowers them for "everything pertaining to life and godliness." A vision of this nature serves to transform believers to do the perfect will of God – not just know it. This is why Prov. 28:19 states when there is "no vision, the people are unrestrained, but happy is he who keeps the law."

This means that without a vision (as described above), the people do not receive direction from God and therefore live spiritually immature, carnal lives (1 Cor. 3:1–3; Heb. 5:11–14). This is why they are unrestrained and why they perish. When the vision of the church is not based on what the head of the church, Christ, wants for His church, the people cast off all restraints and there is no fruit of the Spirit. The people live based on their own rules, and they lack true joy. This is what the people with short-term visions and sometimes no vision experienced in the book of Judges. "In those days there was no king in Israel; everyone did what was right in his own eyes" (Jud. 17:6), was the end result.

When the vision is directed, controlled and empowered by the Word of God, the people are happy; they rejoice ("but happy is he who keeps the law") due to their spiritual maturity that comes as a result of the powerful, transforming work of the Holy Spirit's fruit in their lives. The work of the Holy Spirit is life transforming because it also allows each members of the church to use their spiritual gift (1 Pet. 4:10), which in turns leads to unity as each gift is fitted together for the glory of God (Eph. 4:16). It hearkens back to when the people under Joshua's leadership committed to God's vision directed completely by God's Word (Josh. 1:6–9). They were so empowered and excited over their success, as God had promised Joshua, that at the end of Joshua's days they said: "'We will serve the Lord our God and we will obey His voice.' So Joshua made a covenant with the people that day, and made for them a statute and an ordinance in Shechem" (Josh. 24:24).

These significant accomplishments not only blessed the kingdom of God; they blessed people who are now allowed to live in the land all the days of their lives. It is from the church that Christ impacts the world (Eph. 1:22–23), restrains evil (Matt. 16:17–19; Eph. 3:10), unifies believers (John 17:20–23; 1 Cor. 12), and develops a community of believers who sincerely love one another (John 13:34–35). It is from the church that each believer experiences the inner workings of the Holy Spirit manifested through spiritual gifts that serve the body of Christ (Eph. 2:10; 3:16–17; 1 Pet. 4:10; 1 Cor. 12:4–6). The church, is "suitable for the fullness of times (Eph. 1:10). The properly functioning church will always remain relevant to the changing needs of believers, the neighboring community and the world because Christ designed it "with a view to administration suitable to the fullness of times" (Eph. 1:10). This is why it is imperative that a pastor does not "look to the heavens" and await a vision.

The pastor must search the scriptures for the meaning and intent of the church in order to outline its vision. This way, the pastor lays a foundation that has already been laid, which is Jesus Christ (1 Cor. 3:10–11); it is His body and He is the head. This not only shapes the vision, but it also serves as a way of measuring its validity. If we are careful to implement God's vision biblically, our success is guaranteed (Josh. 1:5–9).

On a football field the quarterback must have vision for the correct play, but player execution ensures that the vision is carried out. God the Father, God the Son, and God the Holy Spirit empowers the church when the pastor He has called to shepherd the flock correctly conveys the plan based on the Word of God. Christ's headship is fully exposed (Col. 1:15–18); the gifts of the Holy Spirit fit the body together perfectly (1 Cor. 12:3–6, 27; Eph. 4:16), and God determines the results (1 Cor. 12:6). This process does not restrain the pastor, it liberates him because it establishes confidence that Christ "has his back."

The Word of God instructs us to worship the Lord regularly (Heb. 10:23–25), but He does not say that it must start at eleven o'clock and the choir must wear a red robe and sing five songs. Christ instructs the pastor to equip the saints, but He does not say that the only way to do this is in

Sunday School. Christ provides us a lot of freedom because the truth does not confine believers; it liberates them (John 8:31–32) from man-made laws.

Sometimes a church does not meet the needs of the people in an effective manner because the man-made structure it implemented became law. Even though many of leaders know that the needs of believers have changed, many churches continue to employ the same methods as if God Himself ordained them. Some churches have the same order of worship, the same programs, year after year with no evaluation of their effectiveness. Some churches hold to traditions because "this is the way we do things here." As a result, believers go through the same routine week after week, wishing someone would do something to break the monotony, and then they assume that because they attend church each week they are right with God.

The church, feeling pressured to create some excitement, develops dynamic worship services and short sermons designed to tickle ears and attract members. So instead of the church being an organism that nurtures and develops believers to spiritual maturity, it becomes a Sunday worship experience.

The same thing happened with our Jewish spiritual ancestors. The Hebrews were provided a system that clearly delineated how they must worship God and live for Him. In an effort to keep everyone on track with the constant pressure from Rome among them, Hebrew leaders, the Pharisees, developed 300 more laws in an effort to protect Judaism from Hellenism. As a result, the people became burdened and soon turned away from God. They began to practice their traditions more than the principles of God. They may not have become controlled by Hellenism, but they did become controlled more by the traditions of the elders rather than the principles of God. The leaders protected the people from Hellenism but not from themselves.

And He said to them, "Rightly did Isaiah prophesy of you hypocrites, as it is written, 'This people honors me with their lips, but their heart is far away from me. But in vain do they worship me, teaching as doctrines the precepts of men.' Neglecting the commandment of God, you hold to the 'tradition of men.'" He was also saying to them, "You are experts at setting aside the commandment of God in order to keep your tradition" (Mark 7:6–9).

See to it that no one takes you captive through philosophy and empty deception, according to the tradition of men, according to the elementary principles of the world, rather than according to Christ. For in Him all the fullness of Deity dwells in bodily form, and in Him you have been made complete, and He is the head over all rule and authority (Col. 2:8–11).

Maybe this is why Paul told Timothy, "Pay close attention to yourself and to your teaching; persevere in these things, for as you do this you will ensure salvation both for yourself and for those who hear you" (1 Tim. 4:16). He said the same after training the leaders in Ephesus, "Be on guard for yourselves and for all the flock, among which the Holy Spirit has made you overseers, to shepherd the church of God which He purchased with His own blood. I know that after my departure savage wolves will come in among you, not sparing the flock; and from among your own selves men will arrive, speaking perverse things, to draw away the disciples after them (Acts 20:28–30)."

## LESSONS FROM JOSHUA

Joshua was given a clear directive from God. He was to go in and possess the land. God gave him instructions on how to cross the Jordan and walk around the walls of Jericho, but Joshua had to now use all he learned under Moses's tutelage. When Joshua decided to go up against Ai (Josh. 8), he put together a war strategy, decided the number of men he would use, told them the direction they needed to go and sent them out. Achan sinned when Joshua and the elders went before God, and God responded as if they should have known what to do. "So the Lord said to Joshua, 'Rise up! Why is it that you have fallen on your face?'" (Josh. 7:10).

After the powerful crossing of Israel through the Jordan and the powerful victory over Jericho, Joshua was surprised that God would allow them to be defeated and God's people embarrassed in this manner. Why would God allow Israel to be defeated and empower their enemies to attack them furiously? Joshua should have known: God said that he would have success if they were careful to obey His Word, and so God seemed surprised that Joshua cannot figure out what went wrong. Again, even though God allowed Joshua the freedom to develop a war strategy, their defeat was not because the strategy did not work; it was because of the sin of Achan. The same is found in the New Testament. If the church is to remain under Christ's headship, it must deal with sin (Matt. 16:16–20; 18:15–21; 1 Cor. 1; 2 Cor. 2:5–11) and this will determine the outcome of the world (1 Pet. 4:17). God cleanses His church, whether or not leaders deal with sin. (1 Cor. 11:27–31).

Again, Joshua had a lot of freedom for organizing how the nation of Israel would take over the Promised Land, but success was determined by their commitment to preserve the Word of God. This is why it is important to develop a vision as the ancient biblical prophets did—given to the congregation directly from His Word, and controlled by the power of the Holy Spirit. We must analyze specifically what Christ wants His church to do (Matt. 16:17) and do it accordingly; this determines the results and empowers the plan.

> Only be strong and very courageous; be careful to do according to all the law which Moses My servant commanded you; do not turn from it to the right or to the left, so that you may have success wherever you go. This book of the law shall not depart from your mouth, but you shall meditate on it day and night, so that you may be careful to do according to all that is written in it; for then you will make your way prosperous, and then you will have success (Josh. 1:7–8).

Leaders must exercise freedom wherever God allows them and submit to God's Word in whatever way God directs them. This is why we are instructed that if we love Him (i.e. keep His commandments, John 14:15) we must follow Him (John 14:27). Before Christ died, He told His disciples,

> Abide in Me, and I in you. As the branch cannot bear fruit of itself unless it abides in the vine, so neither can you unless you abide in Me. I am the vine, you are the branches; he who abides in Me and I in him, he bears much fruit, for apart from Me you can do nothing (John 15:4–6).

To follow Christ is to commit to trust Him, and obey Him to the point of self-denial (Luke 14:26–27; Gal. 2:20; Col. 3:1–4).

Leaders must lead God's saints to Christ instead of man-made laws, human philosophy, or traditions. Visions not based on faith are merely ambitious aspirations which may accomplish much according to the world's standards, but leave believers in an immature state despite their frequent church attendance. The lordship of Christ becomes secondary because believers become trained to enjoy one worship service after another. The church becomes more focused on numbers growth than spiritual growth.

We proclaim Him, admonishing every man and teaching every man with all wisdom, so that we may present every man complete in Christ. For this purpose also I labor, striving according to His power, which mightily works within me (Col. 1:28–29).

Please do not misunderstand me. I am a pastor; I love to see growth. I pray for growth because a flowing stream keeps the stream fresh. However, growing the church cannot be the sole purpose of the church. It should be the end result of seed planted on good soil because when Christ (the Church, the body of Christ, is functioning based on what He prescribes—headship as He directed—spiritual gifts directed by the Holy Spirit—it develops unity and unity creates strength) is lifted up, He increases the numbers.

Day by day continuing with one mind in the temple, and breaking bread from house to house, they were taking their meals together with gladness and sincerity of heart, praising God and having favor with all the people. And the Lord was adding to their number day by day those who were being saved (Acts 2:46–47).

The need for a vision is just as important as the need to have the vision shaped by the powerful Word of God. The powerful result is described in the following verses:

Therefore if there is any encouragement in Christ, if there is any consolation of love, if there is any fellowship of the Spirit, if any affection and compassion, make my joy complete by being of the same mind, maintaining the same love, united in spirit, *intent on one purpose* (Phil. 2:1–2; emphasis mine).

I pray also for those who will believe in me through their message, that *all of them may be one*, Father, just as you are in me and I am in you. May they also be in us so that the world may believe that you have sent Me (John 17:20b–21 NIV; emphasis mine).

## Chapter Two

# A BIBLICAL OVERVIEW OF THE NEW TESTAMENT CHURCH

A s we consider formulating a vision statement, let us first get a bird's-eye view of the New Testament Church. The foundation of the Church is already laid (1 Cor. 3:10–15) and Paul instructs us to build upon it. Therefore, when we outline the vision statement, we must understand the foundation we are instructed to build upon.

### WHAT IS THE CHURCH?

Christ talks about two kinds of churches: the universal church (Matt. 16:18) and the local church (Matt.18:17). Each time, He does not refer to it as an institution, but as an *ekklesia*, meaning an assembly of individuals whom He considered to belong directly to Him. Paul follows His lead, addressing the universal Church in Ephesians 5:23,25 and the local church in 1 Cor. 1:2 and 4:17. Paul states that there are four important qualities that should characterize the Church. They are faith, hope and love with the greatest being love (1 Cor. 13:13); and fidelity to the Word of God, which he states should dwell in believers richly (Col. 3:15–17). Jesus Christ, presented through the Word, must serve as the chief cornerstone (Eph. 2:20). Therefore, the New Testament local church represents a group of baptized believers of Jesus Christ (1 Cor. 1:2; 12:12–14) working together to carry out His, plans, purpose and will (Eph. 1:11). These believers are baptized because they have first by faith accepted as fact that

Christ died for their sins, and secondly have confessed Him as Lord (Rom. 10:9,10; 1 Cor. 1:17).

The believers must gather regularly (1 Cor. 1:2; 11:18; Acts 20:7; Heb. 10:24, 25), for the building up, and equipping of one another (Eph. 4:11–13; 1 Tim. 4:1–16) through teaching, prayer, singing, the Lord's Supper and fellowship (Acts 2:42). This will be done as a result of the use of individual gifts (Rom. 12:3–21; 1 Cor. 12:14; 1 Pet. 4:10), so that believers will be imitators of Christ (Eph. 4:1–2; 5:1–2) to be presented perfect in Him (Col. 1:28–29). These believers must also become witnesses for Christ in the local community and the world (Acts 1:8; 2:42–47; 13:1–4). They must seek to function as one body united in Christ characterized as a loving community for God's glory (Acts 2:44–47; Eph. 2:14–18). Finally, the absolute foundation for developing church ministry must rest on the authority of the Word of God (2 Tim. 3:16; Matt. 4:4; Acts 20:27), and the goal of the ministry must be to disciple (Matt 28:19–2) believers to be mature in Christ (Col. 1:28–29). The church must also bear the responsibility of representing Christ comprehensively before the community (Eph. 1:22).

## THE CHURCH'S IDENTITY

The church finds its identity in Christ. He is the head of it (Col. 1:18) and it is His body (Eph. 1:22). Christ's Helper, the Holy Spirit, shapes His body (1 Cor. 12:4), reminds and guides believers into all truth (John 14:16; 16:13), and fits it together.

Believers must serve in the local church (Eph. 4:12) by way of their spiritual gifts (1 Pet. 4:10; Rom. 12:3–8) in order for the church to functionally demonstrate the body of Christ at work. All those who accept Christ into their lives are representatives of the church in society (Luke 17:11; 1 Cor. 3:16; 2 Cor. 2:14–16; Eph. 3:16–17). These believers no longer live for themselves; they now, as a result of their spiritual maturity, live for Christ and Christ alone.

Please be reminded that I did not say that a person lost their personality; I said they lost their tendency to "live for themselves." A husband and wife do not lose their personalities, but they do become one flesh (Gen. 2:24). Paul had the same zeal and boldness after he met Christ on the road to Damascus and Peter still had the same big mouth. Paul describes this in various letters to the churches:

For the equipping of the saints for the work of service, to the building up of the body of Christ; until we all attain to the unity of the faith, and of the knowledge of the Son of God, to a mature man, to the measure of the stature which belongs to the fullness of Christ. As a result, we are no longer to be children (Eph. 4:12–14).

I have been crucified with Christ; and it is no longer I who live, but Christ lives in me; and the life which I now live in the flesh I live by faith in the Son of God, who loved me and gave Himself up for me (Gal. 2:20).

Therefore if you have been raised up with Christ, keep seeking the things above, where Christ is, seated at the right hand of God. Set your mind on the things above, not on the things that are on earth. For you have died and your life is hidden with Christ in God. When Christ, who is our life, is revealed, then you also will be revealed with Him in glory" (Col. 3:1–4).

## GOD'S WORD

The Word of God, which represents the character and nature of Christ (John 1:1–4), establishes His power on earth (Heb. 1:2–4; 4:12), shapes the vision of the church, and directs and shapes the identity of the church. The Word of God empowers this process in the following manner:

- Adequately equips God's pastors with wisdom and knowledge (2 Tim. 3:16; Jer. 3:15), as a result of diligent studying of the scriptures (2 Tim. 2:15).

- Serves to provide the church its purpose and plans (Matt. 16:17–9; Eph. 1:9–11).

- Strengthens marriages and blesses the development of the family (Eph. 5:22–6:4).

- Protects believers from the attacks of Satan (Matt. 16:19; 1 Cor. 5; 2 Cor. 2:5–11; Eph. 3:10).

- Empowers the church to win lost sheep (Matt. 5:13–16; 28:18–20; Rom. 10:9, 17).

- Equips the saints (Eph. 4:12), and determines how broken lives are repaired.

- Directs the development of a unified body (Eph. 4:13; 1 Cor. 12:4–27).

- Establishes Christ before the community and the world (John 20:22–23; 1 John 4:4; 1 Pet. 4:17).

- Develops believers to be spiritually mature (Eph. 4:12–13; Col. 1:28–29).

- Serves to assist believers to find God's perfect will (Rom. 12:2).

## CHURCH ATTENDANCE: CRITICAL TO IDENTITY

Because worship occurs as a result of the body of Christ gathering together, worship serves as a constant reminder of the identity of the church. The various functions of worship also serve as a reminder of who we live for and who we serve. Worship is on the first day of the week (1 Cor. 16:1–3), representing His resurrection and the Lord's Supper (Acts 20:7). Believers magnify, praise, honor and adore Him, and are reminded that all things function as a result of His being (Col. 1:15–20). Preaching of the Word explains the nature and person of Christ, and challenges believers to stimulate one another to love and good deeds (Heb. 11:23–26).

> They devoted themselves to the apostles' teaching and to fellowship, to the breaking of bread and to prayer. Everyone was filled with awe at the many wonders and signs performed by the apostles. All the believers were together and had everything in common. They sold property and possessions to give to anyone who had need. Every day they continued to meet together in the temple courts. They broke bread in their homes and ate together with glad and sincere hearts... (Acts 2:42–46).

Married and single people alike find their identity in the church, with married couples demonstrating the unique relationship between Christ and the Church. It is like little churches emptying into a bigger church so that all these churches complete the gathering believers for the glory of God.

## DANGER: THE CHURCH APART FROM CHRIST

The church identifying with Christ provides a powerful manifestation of Christ on earth. However, when believers of a local congregation choose to operate independent of Christ, He can choose to remove His lampstand. There are several reasons outlined in Revelation that would lead to Christ removing His presences from the church.

- Believer's lack of love for each other (Rev. 2:4–5). This is significant to the life of a church. Paul says this is the most essential element in a church (1 Cor. 13:3–8). John states that it represents that believers are true disciples of Christ (John 13:34–35), because they are committed to love God by obeying His commands. John continues in 1 John 4:7–12 to inform believers that "anyone who does not love does not know God because God is love."

- False doctrine and "acts of immorality" – the church of Pergamum.

- False doctrine – the church of Thyatira.

- Unfaithful service – the church of Sardis and Laodicea.

## RESPONSIBILITY OF BELIEVERS WITHIN THE CHURCH

Believers' participation in the development of the church's vision is extremely important to the health and strength of the church. When believers did not faithfully serve Christ in the church of Laodicea, because they became enslaved to the riches of this world, Christ decided not to identify with them (Rev. 3:14–18). Believers must not allow themselves to become so absorbed by the world and the cares of the world that they no longer faithfully worship, serve and participate in church activities.

## THE MISSION

Israel's sole purpose was to be God's royal priesthood that would demonstrate His glory to the surrounding nations. "How then, if you will indeed obey My voice and keep My covenant, then you shall be My own possession among all the peoples, for all the earth is Mine; and you shall be to Me a kingdom of priests and a holy nation. These are the words that you shall speak to the sons of Israel" (Exod. 19:5–6). The New Testament Church has the same directive from Christ. "But you are a chosen race, a royal priesthood, a holy nation, a people for God's own possession, so that you may proclaim the excellencies of Him who has called you out of darkness into His marvelous light" (1 Pet. 2:9). Christ's prayer supports this view John 17:20–23) as well as His purpose for creating mankind:

> Worthy are You, our Lord and our God, to receive glory and honor and power; for You created all things, and because of Your will they existed, and were created (Rev. 4:11).

Of the church Paul says:

> And He put all things in subjection under His feet, and gave Him as head over all things to the church, which is His body, the fullness of Him who fills all in all (Eph. 1:22–23).

No church located in any community is there only for the purpose of worship, Sunday School, Bible study, benevolence and door-to-door evangelism from time to time. The church headed by Christ, structurally attached to His body, is there to be a blessing to believers, the community and the world. The church is "the fullness of Him who fills all in all." As a result of God's covenant with Abraham, all nations will be blessed. As a result of the church, all nations experience the powerful transforming work of the blessing.

## THE GOALS OF THE NEW TESTAMENT CHURCH

### *Make Disciples That Will Impact the World*

The church must operate on God's agenda in order to experience God's results (1 Cor. 12:4–7). The primary focus of the church is to make disciples (Matt. 28:19–20; Mark 16:15–16; Acts 1:6–11, Col. 1:28). As a result, all church ministries, programs and structures should be constantly scrutinized to ensure that discipleship is baked into every aspect of the church's life.

Under that overarching mission, the church must develop viable mechanisms to teach God's Word, mend broken lives, renew minds to prioritize God's will, encourage and enable spiritual service, and, most importantly, help believers to act out of love.

Whoever keeps His word, in him the love of God has truly been perfected. By this we know that we are in Him (1 John 2:5).

By this all men will know that you are My disciples, if you have love for one another (John 13:35).

You are the salt of the earth (Matt. 5:13).

### Keep Satan—and Sin Out

When the church was first mentioned by Christ in Matthew 16:18, the focus was to keep Satan out. Paul continues this focus when he warns the elders to keep an eye out for wolves (Acts 20:29). The second time Christ discusses the church was to instruct the disciples how to keep Satan out. Christ outlined this within the framework of accountable relationships.

He also instructed the church to deal with sin. Christ does not leave this entirely on the church's shoulder. He instructs believers to remember the Lord's Supper regularly. "Therefore whoever eats the bread or drinks the cup of the Lord in an unworthy manner, shall be guilty of the body and the blood of the Lord. But a man must examine himself, and in so doing he is to eat of the bread and drink of the cup. For he who eats and drinks, eats and drinks judgment to himself if he does not judge the body rightly. For this reason many among you are weak and sick, and a number sleep. But if we judged ourselves rightly, we would not be judged. But when we are judged, we are disciplined by the Lord so that we will not be condemned along with the world" (1 Cor. 11:27–32).

When a life of holiness or living righteously is discussed in the church, many believers drop their heads as if this is for people who are perfect. This is far from the truth. There are no believers that live perfect lives in Christ. "If we say that we have no sin, we are deceiving ourselves and the truth is not in us" (1 John 1:8).

The issue is not that believers are shaped into a state of perfection. The issue is that believers first, by renewing their minds learn the scriptures they need in order to know what to obey. Secondly, because these believers are committed to obey the truth, their lives become transformed (Rom. 12:2) and the Holy Spirit convicts them when they sin (John 16:7–10). This process allows God's love to be perfected in them and they bear much fruit (1 John 2:3–6; John 15:1–4). These believers that are committed to live righteously (live by the right standards of God) are now slaves to righteousness (Rom. 6:15–18).

It is for this reason that grace abounds (Rom. 5:20–21; 6:1,15). Grace abounds to provide believers the freedom to grow and mature into the fullness of God (Col. 1:9–12; Rom. 8:5–11). This pattern of living out our love for God is a commitment to holiness. Believers that are not committed to this maturation process live carnal lives (1 Cor. 3:1–3) which are no longer controlled or directed by the Holy Spirit.

Abraham by no means was a perfect man. Scripture records several instances of him sinning. But Abraham had a heart to obey God. The more he obeyed God, the more he grew; so that when God required His son to be sacrificed; Abraham could offer him before God.

A young boy who committed his heart to Christ at an early age truly sought to walk with God. But while in junior high school, he started to hang out with the wrong friends. Even though his parents would warn him and did things to prevent him from being around his friends, he persisted. His friends went down to the park one day and got into a fight with another kid and were picked up by the police. Someone thought that he was with his friends so the police arrested him also. This incident brought this young man to his senses and for the first time he realized everything that his parents were trying to say to him. He repented, became more involved in church, began listening to his parents, committed to a discipleship process and over time grew and matured in Christ. His renewed commitment does not mean that this young man never sinned; it just means that he was more committed to obey the Word of God than the desires of the flesh. This young man became a maturing believer benefiting from the grace of God that so freely abounds, because of the righteousness that Christ imputed to him because of his life (Phil. 2:12). And he did it because he was blessed to be part of a church that emphasized discipleship and did not shrink from identifying sin.

### Display Unity

The only time that Christ prayed for the church was when He prayed that the church would be united in Him. "I do not ask on behalf of these alone, but for those also who believe in Me through their word; that they may all be one; even as You, Father, are in Me and I in You, that they also may be in Us, so that the world may believe that You sent me. The glory which You have given Me I have given to them, that they may be one, just as We are one; I in them and

You in Me, that they may be perfected in unity, so that the world may know that You sent Me, and loved them, even as You loved Me" (John 17:20–23). One of the goals of the church is to develop a unified body focused on glorifying God. Unity is achieved as a result of the church's commitment to discipleship. This is clear from Christ's statement in John 17:23: "that they may be one, just as We are one; I in them and You in Me, that they may be perfected in unity."

When Paul addresses unity in Ephesians 4:1, he states the need for believers to "walk in a manner worthy of calling with which they have been called." The calling is in Ephesians 1:4: "He chose us in Him before the foundation of the world, that we would be holy and blameless before Him." Unity achieves holiness and holiness manifested in the life of the assembly of believers leads them to functioning in one Spirit which glorifies God. As a result unity becomes their strength. There are two other key factors that are involved in achieving unity in a church.

The first one is that the church must maintain doctrinal positions that are consistent with God's Word (Tit. 1:9). "There is one body and one Spirit, just as also you were called in one hope of your calling; one Lord, one faith, one baptism, one God and Father of all who is over all and through all and in all" (Eph. 4:3–6). The church should not allow diverse doctrinal positions to exist in one body. It is critical that the discipleship process include correct teaching on God's Word in its historical and grammatical context.

Timothy is warned by Paul:

"O Timothy, guard what has been entrusted to you, avoiding worldly and empty chatter and the opposing arguments of what is falsely called knowledge which some have professed and thus gone astray from the faith" (1 Tim. 6:20–21).

Timothy is also told what causes the church to divide when the doctrine is polluted:

But the Spirit explicitly says that in later times some will fall away from the faith, paying attention to deceitful spirits and doctrines of demons (1 Tim. 4:1–2).

Maybe this is why Titus and others are given instructions to keep an eye on those who cause dissensions, and to even reject such persons (Tit. 3:9–11;

Rom. 16:17–18; 2 Thess. 3:14–15). Paul warned the elders of Ephesus after training them for three years to watch for those who teach false doctrine (Acts 20:29–30).

The second element is service. When believers use their spiritual gift (Eph. 4:7; 1 Pet. 4:10) the Holy Spirit fits them together "fitly" so that the whole body grows into the fullness of God "according to the proper working of each individual part" (Eph. 4:12, 16). A body fitting together fitly obviously leads to a unified body controlled by the Holy Spirit (1 Cor. 12:4–5). The goal of the church is to develop a governing structure that is organized biblically.

The first church was forced to do this because the needs of the church caused them to neglect prayer and the study of the scriptures (Acts 6:1–6). When Paul started the church in Ephesus, he discipled a group of men and trained them to be elders whose job it was to guard the flock. Paul instructed Timothy and Titus to organize a church (Tit. 1:5–9). He told Timothy, "but in case I am delayed, I write so that you will know how one ought to conduct himself in the household of God, which is the church of the living God, the pillar and support of the truth" (1 Tim. 3:15). An organized approach to these things causes the church to function in a cohesive manner even though it is addressing a variety of issues.

Without question, the church will achieve unity when its body is committed to its vision, using spiritual gifts to serve the strategy and loving biblical accountability among believers which all leaders to Christ's lordship over the church. "Therefore if there is any encouragement in Christ, if there is any consolation of love, if there is any fellowship of the Spirit, if any affection and compassion, make my joy complete by being of the same mind, maintaining the same love, united in spirit, intent on one purpose" (Phil. 2:1–2).

Therefore the church's mission is to represent the person and the rule of God in human history.

> Once, having been asked by the Pharisees when the kingdom of God would come, Jesus replied, "The kingdom of God does not come with your careful observation, nor will people say, 'Here it is,' or 'There it is,' because the kingdom of God is within you" (Luke 17:21).

### The Holy Spirit and the Church

It is the Holy Spirit at Pentecost that brought the Church into being, where He first indwelt and empowered individual believers. Christ Himself

30

stated that the disciples would do greater things because of the ministry of the Holy Spirit (John 14:12). The Holy Spirit is essential to the church; He illuminates the Word of God; (John 16:13); distinguishes between a lie and the truth (1 John 2:20–21,27); convicts of sin (John 16:7–8); unifies (Eph. 4:16); and empowers believers to use their spiritual gifts and manifest the fruit of the Spirit. "In Him, you also, after listening to the message of truth, the gospel of your salvation—having also believed, you were sealed in Him with the Holy Spirit of promise" (Eph. 1:13). The Holy Spirit who is the Helper of Christ (John 14:16–17) is focused in the same manner as Christ—mature the church so that the kingdom of God is magnified on earth. The presence of the Holy Spirit is the evidence of a believer's salvation (Matt. 7:16–20), and Christ being with the believers (Rom. 8:9–10). The Holy Spirit makes the church holy and pure (1 Cor. 6:19–20). For just as the temple was holy and sacred place under the old covenant because God dwelt in it, so also are believers sanctified under the new covenant because they are the temple of the Holy Spirit.

Developing clear, biblical approaches to the goal, mission, and ministry of the Holy Spirit is critical to the health and strength of believers as they impact the community and the world (Matt.15:2–3; Mark 7:6–9; Col. 2:8).

## CONCLUSION

The church leadership must convey to believers the foundational mission and goals of the Church as ordained by God in the scripture. It is critical that the Church be focused on God's agenda. If not, it has eliminated its biblical reason for existence.

## Chapter Three

# DESIGNING YOUR CHURCH'S VISION

The purpose of this chapter is to provide a strategy that allows a pastor to construct a vision statement and a clear, multi-year strategic plan for its implementation. The overall focus of this process is to impact the lives of the parishioners and to effectively minister to the diverse needs of the community and the world. A vision provides a ministry with direction. It answers the question, where is the ministry going? It brings the future into focus for both the leader and those who are part of the ministry organization.[1]

The vision statement is a powerful mechanism that impacts every aspect of the church. Everything a church does must find its direction in the vision statement. Everyone must be able to trace activities back to the vision. This includes sermons, ministry structure, staff hiring, budget, church geographical placement and layout, ministry partners, and even the design of materials.

## DEFINITION OF A VISION

Visionary planning is a process by which a church envisions its future and develops the necessary procedures and operations to achieve that future (J. William Pfeiffer).

---

1. Statement about vision adapted from Aubrey Malphurs, *Advanced Strategic Planning* (Grand Rapids: Baker Books, 1999).

A visionary plan is a framework used to carry out strategic thinking, directions, and actions leading to the achievement of consistent and planned results (Patrick J. Below, George L. Morrisey, and Betty Acomb).

A vision is a planned process that structures the future of the church. From the vision, the church can develop a mission statement, goals and objectives for various ministries, a structure that aligns with the vision statement and a time line.

A vision is also something that can be measured. This means that it can be evaluated based on whether or not it is achieving its objectives. It can also be brought back on track if it strays from its original intent. It is not so subjective or vague that its meaning can only be determined by the person who wrote it. It is always clear and can easily be interpreted by any member who reads it. It cannot be so long or exaggerated that it becomes impossible to comprehend or achieve. So it must be within the scope of the ability of the leaders (Exod. 18:21; Matt. 25:14–30), the nature of the church's membership and the needs of the community.

## A PROCESS FOR DEVELOPING THE VISION STATEMENT

It is important first to fast and pray as you start the visioning process, asking for the Lord's guidance. Find a place where no one can disrupt you. Ideally, this will be a room that you can use undisturbed, for about a week.

And I arose in the night, I and a few men with me. I did not tell anyone what my God was putting into my mind to do for Jerusalem and there was no animal with me except the animal on which I was riding (Neh. 2:12).

So I went up at night by the ravine and inspected the wall. Then I entered the Valley Gate again and returned. The officials did not know where I had gone or what I had done; nor had I as yet told the Jews, the priests, the nobles, the officials or the rest who did the work (Neh. 2:15–16).

Nehemiah confessed sin, reminded God of the promises He made to Moses, realizing that God is faithful to His promises. He trusted God to be faithful to His promise and began to devise a plan to help his people. Nehemiah began to devise this plan after much prayer and fasting and he did it first by himself. It is extremely important for God's leader to spend time alone with God first.

Make sure there is no phone or television and you have a large white board, several feet wide and tall. Begin by writing down your Bible-based thoughts about the purpose of the church in your community context. Secondly, write down what you would like to see develop in your church or para-church organization within the next three to five years. Thirdly, determine what you believe are some of the ministry's strengths or weaknesses. Then list the needs of the congregation and the community in which you are situated. Is it a stable community, or a transitional one? What are the demographics? Stable two-parent families? Income levels? Access to transportation?

Next, list all of the present ministries of the church and grade their effectiveness from one to ten. After you have listed all of this information, turn your back to the white board and walk out of the room. Come back the next day and do the same thing. Turn your back and leave for a week.

While you are gone from it, make sure no one uses the room. During this week, ask yourself the following important questions: How does the congregation view me as their pastor (or president if you are a para-church organization; Matt. 16:13–16)? Evaluate your own strengths and weaknesses. What is the present vision of the church? If there is not a vision, ask someone—man or woman—in leadership (must have been in the church for at least five to seven years), a person of integrity, about their thoughts about a vision for the church/ministry? When you have gotten answers to these questions, go back to the board and then answer the following questions: Why does this particular church exist (you may end up listing the present status of the church or an old vision statement)? Where are we going (the answer to this may impact your mission statement) and how do we get there (action steps)? Once all these things are completed, check your notes and thoughts against scripture for validity.

Now that you have your notes on the white board, begin checking off all the things you see as critical. Make sure the list includes things that represent your passion—those things that energize you and will therefore compel you to energize the congregation.

> When I heard these words, I sat down and wept and mourned for days; and
> I was fasting and praying before the God of heaven (Neh. 1:4–5).

Nehemiah was intent on one purpose. No one had to tell him what to do. He was not assigned to do this job; instead, his ministry grew out of a compassion for hurting people that developed into his passion. When the heart of the leader is surrendered to God, their compassion and passion, through the influence of the Holy Spirit, is nurtured and shaped by God. That is the most powerful way for a leader to lead.

Next, indicate which ministries should remain and what ministries need to be developed to fulfill the vision.

Now you can match your list against the church's strengths and weaknesses and collapse your notes into one cohesive ministry vision statement. Put the statement down for a week and spend time in prayer. Get the statement and rewrite it several times until it comprehensively and succinctly presents the results of your research. The vision statement must be specific enough to understand its intent, but broad enough for the vision to expand over a period of time. This allows for flexibility and a greater level of efficiency for its development and evolution over time.

When you have finished all the research, prayer time and writing, invite in some of your staff, ministry leaders and church leaders and ask them what they believe the vision statement is saying. When leaders feel a part of something, they tend to be more involved in the implementation of it. If they struggle with some of the words and do not understand some of the statements, allow them to have input. Once they have finished the initial discussion, collaborate on a final agreed-upon statement. Ask them to pray about it. Then, invite them back for another meeting to do one more reading.

Your process here is important. Invite the elders first, as biblically they have spiritual responsibility for the congregation (Acts 20:28–30; 1 Tim. 6:20–21). Deacons are next, then ministry leaders and department heads. Follow this order for the next set of activities as well.

## PROCESS FOR DEVELOPING THE MISSION STATEMENT

The mission statement provides a general summary of how the church plans on implementing the vision. You will want to consider what major ministry areas are represented in the vision statement and how they relate to the vision. Then, you will develop a mission statement that delineates these various ministries. Ensure that the mission supports the vision, and that it is biblically consistent with Christ's directive to the church.

Here is an example of a mission statement from my own church:

Living Word Fellowship Church is a non-denominational church that is focused on cultivating a unified community of believers of our Lord Jesus

Christ, by establishing and equipping believers to care for each other and serve the Lord through the ministries of the church. These ministries include Worship, Shepherding Ministry, Discipleship, Children and Youth Ministry, Ministries through the Christian Outreach Center, Evangelism and Missions Ministry, Fellowship Ministry, and Family Ministry. This process operates under authority of the inerrant Word of God, which is illuminated through the ministry of the Holy Spirit. The outreach and missions ministries will serve to impact the neighboring community, as well as around the world.

## DEVELOPING A MOTTO FOR THE CHURCH
Once the vision statement and the mission statement are complete, develop a motto. This is a way of providing a "vision at a glance" for the congregation. The motto for the church that I pastor is "United in Christ to Impact the World."

Think through what is the overall intent and goal of the vision statement. Pick key words from the statement and list them. Once you have listed them, evaluate which words you or your group of ministry leaders conclude best describe the intent and goal of the church. Once this is completed, try to arrange the words in a sentence so that it is easy to remember. Make sure it is not long; it should not be more than seven words.

Test your motto with a few members with varying durations of membership. Ask them what their initial reaction to the motto. Ask them to read the vision and mission statement, and weigh in on consistency with the motto. After you have completed your research, review the suggestions with your ministry heads. Do this on the same white board, which you should have left intact with your notes. Finally, leave it for a little while. During this time, test it with non-church members in your community. Now you can finalize the motto, based on the inputs of many.

## THE ROLE OF CHURCH LEADERSHIP
Church leadership is there to provide advice and counsel. There is one caveat though, if the vision and mission do not violate God's Word, the elders and other leaders should not make suggestions that change the original intent of the plans presented by the pastor. Like Jethro said to Moses in Exodus 18:19–20, and Paul said to Timothy in 1 Tim. 3:15; "but in case I am delayed, I write so that you will know how one ought to conduct himself in the household of God, which is the church of the living God, the pillar and

support of the truth." Paul said this after he instructed him who to choose as elders and deacons. He could have said, "I wanted you, the elders and deacons to know." Instead, Paul said that he wanted Timothy to know, placing the implementation of the plan into Timothy's hands. Paul instructs Titus in the same manner (Tit. 2:15).

The Old Testament demonstrates the same principle. In Numbers 11, the people wanted meat rather than the same diet God had provided. God told Moses to get the elders and officers that he knows are faithful and bring them before God at the tent of meeting. God said that as soon as Moses does what He told him to do, "I will come down and speak with you there" (Num. 11:17). Notice God did not say 'I will come down and speak with everyone there.' This is because Moses needed to share the load. Even though leaders are in place to provide leadership, they must do so to share the pastor's load that God has placed on him as he serves God faithfully.

After consulting with the elders, the pastor should caucus with the deacons. Again, he should stay open to their input and counsel.

As he develops the strategy and execution, the pastor should begin to involve the associate pastors and staff as they will be involved with implementation. Consider this, the men that were with Nehemiah did not come to know the plan until he had a good understanding of how he planned to implement it. In the same way that Nehemiah secured authority from King Artaxerxes to carry out his plan to rebuild Jerusalem's walls, so is the pastor authorized by God to shepherd his flock (Eph. 4:11; Jer. 3:15—"I will give you shepherds..."). Christ must call a pastor because He is the head of the church (Col. 1:18).

After Nehemiah knew what he was about to do, he shared it with the other leaders. "Then I said to them, 'You see the bad situation we are in, that Jerusalem is desolate and its gates burned by fire. Come, let us rebuild the wall of Jerusalem so that we will no longer be a reproach. I told them how the hand of my God had been favorable to me and also about the king's words which he had spoken to me.' Then they said, 'Let us arise and build.' So they put their hands to the good work" (Neh. 2:17–19). Nehemiah was a cupbearer. He was not a city planner or a wall builder. He was the visionary. He was the one with the plan and how to implement it. Nehemiah was not adequate in himself to do or orchestrate every dynamic of the plan. No pastor is adequate to do everything. Paul states in 2 Corinthians 3:5: "Not that we are adequate in ourselves to consider anything as coming from ourselves, but our adequacy is from God."

## WHEN THE PASTOR IS NOT A STRONG LEADER

Some pastors are good shepherds and Bible teachers, but may not have the gift of leadership or the ability to articulate and implement a vision. Nevertheless, it is not biblical for other church leaders to usurp the pastor's leadership. Elders and deacons are chosen, but a pastor is called by Christ, the Head of the Church (Eph. 1:22–23; 4:11).

When Paul was mentoring leaders, he didn't mentor a group. He mentored the one who was to serve as pastor. He wrote to Timothy "so that you may know how one ought to conduct himself in the household of God, which is the church" (1 Tim. 3:15). He did not write to the elders or the deacons. Timothy was a young man, and so Paul had to instruct him not to allow members of the church to disrespect him because he was young (1 Tim. 4:12). Timothy would not necessarily be considered a "strong leader" today; he was timid and had to be encouraged to be strong in faith based on the Word of God (1 Cor. 16:10–11; 2 Tim. 1:7).

We find this same attitude being communicated to Titus. He is told to appoint leaders (1:5), silence rebellious teachers (1:10–11) and "reprove them severely" (1:13). Titus is told to "…speak and exhort and reprove with all authority. Let no one disregard you" (2:15; 3:8). He is told to remind the people how to function in society (3:1–3). Titus is provided direction to; "let our people also learn to engage in good deeds to meet pressing needs, that they may not be unfruitful" (3:14). He was given authority to direct the church.

It is important to respect God's structure when leaders decide that there is a need for a church to have a vision. When the pastor does not demonstrate a desire to establish the church's vision, a few leaders should approach him respectfully about the matter and offer to work directly with him and follow the process outlined above. They should select a few loyal, faithful members to work alongside the pastor during the initial visioning process. After this is done, with much prayer and some fasting, they must allow him to be the one who presents it to the leadership for their evaluations, stepping back when the pastor is prepared to move forward.

## CONCLUSION

A church without a vision is like a ship without a rudder. The ship may move, but it will run aground again and again. The sermons will go from Sunday to Sunday without purpose or direction.

A vision will provide for the people what God wants to do in that local body through His shepherd and leaders, so that each person becomes impacted for the glory of God and so that they in turn will reach others in the surrounding community. Without this dynamic process, unity in the body will be difficult and the leadership of the pastor can be eroded and eventually questioned. A church must have vision or the people will perish!

## Chapter Four

# PROCEEDING FROM VISION
# TO STRATEGY DEVELOPMENT

With a clear vision and the rudiments of a plan, the elders and deacons can support the vision and move forward to strategy development. When deacons or elders are not supportive—this sometimes happens when their membership predates the pastor's—some pastors design ministry boards to maneuver through the conflict. This is not wise, because it infuses a new group with authority that may clash with lay leaders or the ministerial staff.

The pastor then ends up with too many people in authority, and "You cannot serve two masters" (Matt. 6:24). If a pastor has pushback from existing church leadership, he needs to befriend them and let Romans 14:19 be his guide, "So then let us pursue the things which make for peace and the building up of one another."

Abraham Lincoln was accused of meeting too much with the enemy. His leaders asked why? Lincoln told them that the best way to kill your enemy is to make him your friend. When there are control issues, the pastor should have short Bible studies before the board meetings. Keep it within 30 minutes unless the group wants to go longer. Pick books of the Bible to study, or maybe a good book on discipleship. It's hard to argue, or exhibit bitterness, with an open Bible in one's hand!

Holding Bible study classes with elders and deacons does not mean all the elders or deacons will support every part of the implementation process.

It will, however, lead to a board that is more spiritually mature, more committed to scripture, more open to discipleship and more dependent on the Lord for direction. When leaders learn to be followers of Christ, the spiritual influence of God leads to all things becoming more productive for His glory and honor (1 Cor. 12:4–8).

Even the Apostle Paul had a difficult time being accepted by the disciples. After escaping through an opening in the wall in Damascus, Paul went to Jerusalem to spend time with the disciples, but they did not readily accept him:

> When he came to Jerusalem, he was trying to associate with the disciples; but they were all afraid of him, not believing that he was a disciple. But Barnabas took hold of him and brought him to the apostles and described to them how he had seen the Lord on the road, and that He had talked to him, and how at Damascus he had spoken out boldly in the name of Jesus. And he was with them, moving about freely in Jerusalem, speaking out boldly in the name of the Lord. And he was talking and arguing with the Hellenistic Jews; but they were attempting to put him to death. But when the brethren learned of it, they brought him down to Caesarea and sent him away to Tarsus (Acts 9:26–30).

The Apostle Paul did not associate with the disciples regularly, especially since they did not readily accept his call to the Gentiles. He had a vision that had to be confirmed to the first leaders of the Church by Jesus Christ Himself before it was actually implemented (Acts 10:1–23):

> And he said to them, "You yourselves know how unlawful it is for a man who is a Jew to associate with a foreigner or to visit him; and yet God has shown me that I should not call any man unholy or unclean" (Acts 10:28).

> Opening his mouth, Peter said: "I most certainly understand now that God is not one to show partiality, but in every nation the man who fears Him and does what is right is welcome to Him" (Acts 10:34–35).

Finally, Peter understood. Paul ended up staying in Tarsus for 14 years, preaching to the Gentiles:

> Then after an interval of fourteen years I went up again to Jerusalem with Barnabas, taking Titus along also. It was because of a revelation that I went

up; and I submitted to them the gospel which I preach among the Gentiles, but I did so in private to those who were of reputation, for fear that I might be running, or had run, in vain (Gal. 2:1–2).

It is Paul's going up to Jerusalem, as a way of confirming his ministry ("for fear that I might be running, or had run, in vain"), that led to Peter's vision and visit to Cornelius's house along with his fellow travelers (Acts 10:45). God prepared the leader of the disciples for Paul's visit, to lead the other disciples to accept Paul's call, and as a result, they commissioned Paul to go to the Gentiles:

> . . . And recognizing the grace that had been given to me, James and Cephas and John, who were reputed to be pillars, gave to me and Barnabas the right hand of fellowship, so that we might go to the Gentiles and they to the circumcised (Gal. 2:9).

The Jerusalem Council became convinced as a direct result of Peter's experience.

> And I remembered the word of the Lord, how He used to say, "John baptized with water, but you will be baptized with the Holy Spirit." Therefore if God gave to them the same gift as He gave to us also after believing in the Lord Jesus Christ, who was I that I could stand in God's way? When they heard this, they quieted down and glorified God, saying, "Well then, God has granted to the Gentiles also the repentance that leads to life" (Acts 11:16–18).

Paul became fully accepted by the disciples, and released to do ministry in more places than Tarsus as a direct result of God's goodness. Paul did not try to create another group of disciples that approved of his ministry. Instead, he patiently waited on the established structure that Christ put in place, to affirm his call and mission.

Paul had two things to overcome: his past and his vision. By the grace of God, he overcame both. This was God's vision, and God found a way.

The Church must follow this same principle. The process may take longer, but it produces more fruit and a greater level of support. During the waiting period, I am sure that Paul grew and became a better minister, a better leader and gained a greater understanding of God's Word, like David who became a better leader and built a strong army while running from Saul. Pastors and church leaders alike must give the process ample time, and allow the Holy Spirit to guide them into one accord.

When the vision has been presented and the leaders have largely adopted it, there are "next steps" that need to be put in place. The first thing that must be done is to allow the elders and deacons to go back to functioning in their roles (View the "Sheep & Ministry Development" chart in the Appendix) and begin focusing more attention on the associate pastors, ministry leaders, and staff for the implementation of the vision. Secondly, begin analyzing the vision to determine what are the key areas mentioned in the vision statement. For example, at Living Word Fellowship Church, the key areas are Worship, Discipleship, Children and Youth, Fellowship, Outreach, Evangelism and Missions, Family Ministry, Shepherding Ministry, and Administration. Determining what each ministry must be to implement the vision is significant to the development of the overall strategy. Thirdly, once you have decided the key areas, you need to provide a biblical outline for the meaning of each area (Living Word Fellowship Church's ministry outlines can be found in the next chapter). This outline determines the parameters for the individuals who lead the various ministry areas and provides direction for structure. This also keeps things objective when there is conflict.

## BALANCING VISION AND WORK

In the development of the vision it is best to maintain the order of the church. Engage the leadership, but don't have so many meetings that they are overwhelmed and cannot take care of their ongoing ministry responsibilities.

This way, the elders fulfill their God-ordained roles in overseeing the implementation of the Word of God into the life of the church (Acts 1:1–3; 20:27–32). Likewise, deacons continue to care for the flock, and hurting members do not go lacking. Use deacon meetings to keep them updated on the process and give them opportunity to provide input. If your church has deacons but no elders, pick a few lead deacons who can serve like Peter, James, and John did with Christ.

The associate pastors, who assist the pastor with the implementation of the vision, can spend significant time with the pastor as he develops the major areas of the vision. This allows individuals who eventually oversee the ministries of the church to slowly gain ownership of each ministry. Allow lay church members who are financial professionals to work with the pastor to develop the church's budget based on the strategy. View the Appendix charts "Sheep & Ministry Development" and "Deacon Ministry." These charts illustrate how the elders, deacons and caregivers (believers with the gift of encouragement and mercy; Rom. 12:4–8) should maintain a focus on caring for the flock. Follow the example of Paul in Acts 20:27–30, he focused on the development of leaders (he told Timothy to do the same thing when he became a pastor), but Timothy and Titus focused more on the development and furtherance of the ministry that God called the Apostle Paul to do (Acts 16:1–5).

The Old Testament has a similar leadership model. Moses focused on developing elders and judges for the caring of God's flock whereas Joshua was more focused on supporting Moses with non-priestly duties (Exod. 18:17–23; Num. 11:16–17). Joshua's leadership structure patterns a military administration because he focused on entering the Promised Land and taking possession of it. The same thing takes place in the book of Nehemiah. When Nehemiah was rebuilding the wall, nobles, officials, captains were mentioned as leaders. In Nehemiah 8, when the wall was completed and the people wanted to hear the Word of God read, the leaders who served the people were priests, scribes and Levites.

When developing the strategy for implementing the vision of the church, it is important for the church to continue caring for the flock and serving the ministry areas that are functionally in place. When the flock feels neglected, it is hard for them to listen to a plan that is yet to impact their lives.

## ASSOCIATE PASTORS AND MINISTERS

When I talk about associate pastors, the question asked often by members of smaller churches, is what is the difference between ministers and associate pastors? Ministers are individuals who, by their very title, are servants (Mark 10:41–44). Their job is first to be trained (Acts 16:1–5; 2 Tim. 2:15; 3:17), and like Timothy, Titus, and John Mark, serve the needs of the church as it relates to the various ministries which serve the development of the body of Christ (1 Cor. 12). Associate pastors function in the same manner – the only difference is that they work closely with the pastor *to lead the major ministries of the church*. Each associate pastor is a mature believer that meets the requirements of 1 Timothy 3:1–7.

These individuals should go through the same training process as the ministers and should have at least Bible college training and at best seminary training. The reason for this is the more equipped they are, the more efficient and productive the church becomes. They bring insight to the ongoing development of the vision which serves to expand and propel the church in a productive manner. It is important that they remain loyal to the pastor and committed to the vision so that the church does not become disjointed and begin competing against itself. When this occurs, members suffer and the community ends up with a motionless church on another street corner.

An associate pastor should be someone who can serve as a great role model to other ministers by his life, teaching, leadership and his respect for the pastor. This minister should view his function as assisting the pastor in developing and expanding the vision of the church. He must not view himself as doing this for elders, deacons or church members, only for the pastor. When a minister sees himself as carrying out anyone else's vision, it leads to a dysfunctional leadership structure with dissipation of loyalty and confused, conflicted priorities. Remember what took place with John Mark:

> After some days Paul said to Barnabas, "Let us return and visit the brethren in every city in which we proclaimed the word of the Lord, and see how they are." Barnabas wanted to take John, called Mark, along with them also. But Paul kept insisting that they should not take him along who had deserted them in Pamphylia and had not gone with them to the work. And there occurred such a sharp disagreement that they separated from one another, and Barnabas took Mark with him and sailed away to Cyprus. But Paul chose Silas and left, being committed by the brethren to the grace of the Lord (Acts 15:36–40).

This is why Christ warns against pleasing men and Paul follows the example.

> Do not fear those who kill the body but are unable to kill the soul; but rather fear Him who is able to destroy both soul and body in hell (Matt. 10:28–29).

> For am I now seeking the favor of men, or of God? Or am I striving to please men? If I were still trying to please men, I would not be a bond-servant of Christ (Gal. 1:10).

When someone seeks to please men, they can displease God and the vision and loyalty to leadership go right out the door. This is exactly what happened with Peter in Galatians. He desired to please his Jewish brothers, so when they showed up Peter decided to leave the Gentiles and go hang out with the Jews (Gal. 2:11–14). Paul confronted Peter openly because he knew Peter understood what the Lord had showed in Acts 14 and 15. He was concerned that Peter, in his desire to please men, was about to destroy Christ's vision to spread the church worldwide.

## CRYSTALLIZING THE VISION
## FOR MINISTRY DEVELOPMENT

The first thing that needs to be completed is a critical analysis of the vision statement. Let me give you an example. Here is the vision statement of Living Word Fellowship Church:

> The vision of Living Word Fellowship Church is to develop a *community of believers* of Jesus Christ who, through the development of genuine relationships, based on love and truth, will unite for worship focused on glorifying God, through the power of the Holy Spirit, so that everyone will demonstrate faith, hope and love as in 1 Thess. 1:2–3. This church *equips* and *establishes these believers* to function under the authority of the inerrant Word of God. Living Word Fellowship Church also provides viable mechanisms and training programs to empower believers to *reach unbelievers comprehensively* as a local church, as well as corporately with other churches, so that together we impact the *community and the world for God's glory*.

Review your vision statement and highlight the objectives that advance the vision. Once this evaluation is complete and you have decided what your objectives are, create titles for each of these objectives. Here is an example of how this process is implemented at Living Word Fellowship Church.

Every ministry area addresses back to a phrase in the vision statement. The Fellowship Ministry addresses "genuine relationships." The Discipleship and Shepherding Ministries address "church equips" and "establishing these believers." The Family Ministry addresses "community of believers." The Outreach and Evangelism/Missions Ministries address "reach unbelievers comprehensively." Finally, the Administration Ministry addresses the phrase "functioning for the glory of God." It means that we do things decently and in order—the purpose of the Administration Ministry. When the associate pastors do a good job overseeing all these ministry areas, they allow the pastor to truly do the job of an overseer.

Once these objectives have been established, it becomes important that they are biblically defined so that they serve the vision as the vision continues to serve God's purposes for God's church. A pastor must remember that he is a facilitator of God's vision. He is the quarterback that follows the playbook (the Bible). He is not the owner. I have provided charts in the Appendices that outline how these ministries work at Living Word Fellowship Church.

## THE TRADITIONAL CHURCH

Some churches may view these categories as too much of a radical change. This is especially true in churches where a good percentage of the members are seniors and a good percentage of the deacons are seniors. Please remember that by the time the vision is being implemented, the process in this book has gained some support with at least some of the deacons. The actual implementation of the vision however may surprise them. They may not have anticipated the change that would come upon the church as the vision unfolds and begins to change the dynamics of the overall church ministries. They may ask questions: "What does this mean to my ministry area? Does my function get cancelled? Will I have to change the way that I function within the church?" These questions create anxiety and tension for dedicated church workers and leaders. When they hear of the changes, all some leaders think about is whether or not they will keep their position. For some retired people, their ministry provides them an outlet, and for some it goes as far (because their children live a long ways from them) as providing them meaning and a sense of worth, because they have a group of people depending on them. It is the one place they hoped would see them as worth something therefore not dispose of them.

This concern must not be taken lightly because some of the seniors may have been at church for a long time and have truly been faithful.

To avoid these anxieties, make sure that existing ministries fit into one of the main ministry areas that are selected as a result of the Vision Statement. When training the associate pastors for their area of ministry, direct them to meet with lay leaders serving in the existing ministries that are a part of their major ministry area. Direct them to spend time teaching on the vision of the church and the biblical outline of their particular ministry. They should allow ample time for discussion or questions.

The effectiveness of some of the faithful individuals must also be respected. Direct that all lay leaders can maintain their positions if they commit to regularly attending Bible study, Sunday School, special leadership training sessions and worship.

Others who may have grown accustomed to going to the pastor to have everything decided will often want to know "Why can't I talk to the pastor directly? Why do I have to talk with someone else?" The pastor must remain friendly and sympathetic, and with kindness persistently refer them to their ministry leaders. The pastor defeats sharing the load of the ministry, and undermines the leadership of the associate pastors if he continually allows people to come to him for every decision.

All ministries struggle with these issues. It is critical that pastor skillfully, firmly and compassionately deal with people who resist change. He must resist the temptation to alter a God-given vision to a powerful, vocal minority—or majority! If a pastor worries more about losing his job and he decides to protect it, he may maintain his job but lose God's vision for the church.

> And Jesus answered them, saying, "The hour has come for the Son of Man to be glorified. Truly, truly, I say to you, unless a grain of wheat falls into the earth and dies, it remains alone; but if it dies, it bears much fruit. He who loves his life loses it, and he who hates his life in this world will keep it to life eternal. If anyone serves Me, he must follow Me; and where I am, there My servant will be also; if anyone serves Me, the Father will honor him" (John 12:23–26).

## Chapter Five

# MOVING FROM VISION TO MINISTRY

This chapter highlights the ministry outlines that we use at Living Word Fellowship Church. These outlines are an expansion of the vision statement based on the objectives. They are then used to shape the ministry charts that functionally outline each ministry area (see Appendix charts). Each associate pastor must work from these biblical outlines and the charts to implement the vision into the life of the church. If the associate pastor wants to add to the ministry charts, he must do so based on the biblical outlines for each ministry area in consultation with the pastor.

In order to explain this process, I will revisit the vision statement, then provide the outlines based on how the vision statement requires them to flow.

The vision of Living Word Fellowship Church is to develop a *community of believers* of Jesus Christ who, through the development of *genuine relationships*, based on love and truth, will unite for *worship* focused on glorifying God, through the power of the Holy Spirit, so that everyone will demonstrate faith, hope and love as in 1 Thess. 1:2–3. This church *equips* and *establishes* these believers to function under the authority of the inerrant Word of God. Living Word Fellowship Church also provides viable mechanisms and training programs to empower believers to *reach unbelievers comprehensively* as a local church, as well as corporately with other churches, so that together we impact the *community and the world for God's glory.*

Please remember how each objective relates to a ministry area. Here is a quick review:

- Community of believers—Family Ministry and the Shepherding Ministry

- Genuine relationships—Fellowship Ministry

- Worship—Worship Ministry

- The church equipping process—Discipleship Ministry and Children & Youth Ministry

- Reaching unbelievers in the community and world—Outreach Ministry and Evangelism/Missions Ministry.

- Maintaining an orderly process in all these things—Administration Ministry.

Each ministry outline is done from a purely exegetical evaluation of the Word of God. They have no particular denominational influences. It is my desire to assist in exposing God's will for His church, so that it functions in line with His directives. His headship is essential to experiencing His blessings (Rev. 2 & 3).

## MINISTRY OUTLINES
Here are biblical descriptions for the following ministry areas:
Family Ministry
Shepherding Ministry
Fellowship Ministry
Worship Ministry
Discipleship Ministry
Children and Youth Ministry
Outreach Ministry

Evangelism and Missions Ministry
Administration Ministry

## THE BIBLICAL PHILOSOPHY OF THE FAMILY MINISTRY

The family is the foundation upon which God built everything. He created a family in the Garden of Eden (Gen. 1:26–28) and it is from this family that God expected man to rule the earth. This concept extends itself to the church (Eph. 5:32), and Christ is committed to the church (Eph. 1:22–23). Paul tells us in Eph. 5:32 that the husband and wife functioning together represents Christ and the Church, and in verse 26 of the same chapter, the husband is biblically responsible to wash his wife with the Word. This is why the same writer says that if a woman has a question about the Word of God, she must go home and ask her husband (1 Cor. 14:34–35).

Paul also instructs us that a man must rule his home well before he is qualified to be a leader in the church (1 Tim. 3:4–5). The strength of the family determines the strength of the church. When the church, which represents the body of Christ is strong, Christ is lifted up and this allows men and women to be drawn to him.

### Ministry Mission

This ministry will seek to minister to the diverse needs of families. The focus is to grow the family members closer to God and to each other. This ministry will seek to outline the biblical roles of the family and challenge all members of the family to support God's rule for the home. It provides counseling as well as financial planning for all families who seek assistance from this ministry area. This ministry serves as the counseling center for all issues presented to church leadership.

### Activities of the Family Ministry

- Challenge couples to make Christ first in their lives (Luke 12:31). "But seek for His kingdom, and these things shall be added to you."

- Keep fathers and mothers focused on living out the biblical roles God provided them: "And he will restore the hearts of the fathers to their children, and the hearts of the children to their fathers, lest I come and smite the land with a curse."

- Create an environment that allows couples to openly deal with parenting issues. This includes single parent homes.

- Challenge couples that are having problems to attend the marriage class in Life Application and be available for counseling either through the Family Ministry or the Guidance Ministry.

- Encourage couples to attend activities that are a part of the Family Ministry or Fellowship Ministry as outlined in the Family Ministry organizational chart.

- Encourage couples to establish relationships as a result of the Family Ministry activities so that they can become a support to each other.

- Work with couples considering divorce to find godly solutions.

## THE BIBLICAL PHILOSOPHY
## OF THE SHEPHERDING MINISTRY

There is no question that the Bible expects a pastor to provide leadership for the overall development of the body of Christ, the Church. The pastor must do as Moses was instructed to do by Jethro "make known to them the way in which they are to walk, and the work they are to do" (Exod. 18:20). He must know the vision that God has laid on his heart and must organize the work to be done to get the vision implemented into the life of the church.

The pastor must make sure that God's sheep are equipped (Eph. 4:12), trained to apply their spiritual gift (1 Pet. 4:10) and to serve the ongoing development of the body of Christ (Eph. 4:12, 1 Cor. 12). This process must function in an orderly manner for the glory of God (1 Tim. 3:15). All of this must be established based on what God intends for the church as directed by Christ who is the head of the Church (Col. 1:18). This is essential because the Church must operate based on the Word of God, the pillar and foundation of truth (1 Tim. 3:15). Once laid, this is the only foundation that can be laid so that Christ's headship is realized each and every day in the life of the church.

As a result, the pastor is the primary preacher and teacher of God's Word (1 Tim. 5:17) so that the Word being the foremost authority, ("teach them to observe all that I commanded you…", Matt. 28:20; 1 Tim. 4:6; 2 Tim. 4:1–5), guides the life of each believer (1 Cor. 3:10). As a result of this focus each believer is held accountable to Christ for the glory of God. With this kind of leadership the pastor is instructed to organize without fear (2 Tim. 1:7), without strife (2 Tim. 2:14, 23–26), and with the help of elders, deacons, associate pastors, ministers, administrative staff and lay leaders. The leadership that the pastor provides affects the overall development of the church.

> I am writing these things to you, hoping to come to you before long; but in case I am delayed, I write so that you will know how one ought to conduct himself in the household of God, which is the church of the living God, the pillar and support of the truth (1 Tim. 3:14–15).

Notice that even though Paul just mentioned elders and deacons, he told Timothy that he expected the church to operate orderly because of Timothy's leadership ("I am writing these things to you…"). This ministry allows pastoral leadership to influence every other ministry of the church. When this is done biblically, the headship of Christ is established for God's glory. The pastor is instructed not to do this alone because this wears him out (Exod. 18:18); causes believers to not be at peace when they function within the church (Exod. 18:23); and gives Satan a foothold to infiltrate the church (Acts 20:27–32).

This is clearly modeled in Numbers 11. The people are unhappy because they eat the same food every day and they wanted to eat some of the things they had grown used to in Egypt. Moses's expression demonstrates how tired he had become because of how difficult the issues were: "…Thou hast laid the burden of all this people on me?" (Num. 11:16–17). As a result, the pastor needs to train these men (Acts 20:27; 1 Tim. 3:10), and prepare them to effectively serve God's sheep.

> The Lord therefore said to Moses, "Gather for Me seventy men from the elders of Israel, whom you know to be the elders of the people and their officers and bring them to the tent of meeting, and let them take their stand there with you. Then I will come down and speak with you there, and I will take of the Spirit who is upon you, and will put Him upon them; and they shall bear the burden of the people with you, so that you will not bear it all alone. Say to the people, 'Consecrate yourselves for tomorrow, and you shall eat meat; for you have wept in the ears of the Lord, saying, "Oh that someone would give us meat to eat! For we were well-off in Egypt." Therefore the Lord will give you meat and you shall eat'" (Num. 11:16–19).

Notice these are men that Moses knows to be elders, not elders that the other elders may know to be elders (Tit. 1:5). Also God would come and speak to Moses, not to all the elders, and it is the Spirit that is upon Moses that is placed on the other leaders. The discipling of leaders through this ministry is key to helping the pastor share the load of the ministry.

The primary purpose of elders and deacons is to care for God's flock. The caring of God's flock is something that God does not take lightly (Ezek. 34). Caring for God's flock is not just overseeing parishioners to make sure they remain pure in the life of the church (elders' major function), but also helps the weak, as well as those who are sick (deacons' major function). Because the gift of encouragement, mercy, and service is not only for elders and deacons, the church must seek to get lay leaders involved in caring for the flock.

> We urge you, brethren, admonish the unruly, encourage the fainthearted, help the weak, be patient with everyone. See that no one repays another with evil for evil, but always seek after that which is good for one another and for all people (1 Thess. 5:14–19).

These individuals, even though they are called by Christ by way of the Holy Spirit to employ their gift (1 Cor. 12:4–8; 1 Pet. 4:10), must be equipped to this work of service. This team of believers assists the pastor in caring for God's flock so that in the midst of a perverse generation they can find strength to live for the glory of God (Phil. 2:12–18).

> Therefore, I exhort the elders among you, as your fellow elder and witness of the sufferings of Christ, and a partaker also of the glory that is to be revealed, shepherd the flock of God among you, exercising oversight not under compulsion, but voluntarily, according to the will of God; and not for sordid gain, but with eagerness; nor yet as lording it over those allotted to your charge, but proving to be examples to the flock. And when the Chief Shepherd appears, you will receive the unfading crown of glory (1 Pet. 5:1–4).

This ministry is not only focused on training elders and deacons, but also lay leaders for the work of service. It is important for the body of Christ to care for each member as each member uses their spiritual gift.

But now there are many members, but one body. And the eye cannot say to the hand, "I have no need of you." On the contrary, it is much truer that the members of the body which we deem less honorable, on these we bestow more abundant honor, and our less presentable members of the body which we deem less honorable, on these bestow more abundant honor, and our less presentable members become much more presentable. Whereas our more presentable members have no need of it. But God has so composed the body, giving more abundant honor to that member which lacked, so that there may be no division in the body, but that the members may have the same care for one another. And if one member suffer with it; if one member is honored, all the members rejoice with it (1 Cor. 12:20–26).

This ministry must coordinate this work so that the leaders and lay leaders work for the common good of caring for God's flock. "But to each one is given the manifestation of the Spirit for the common good" (1 Cor. 12:7). Modeling this form of leadership in the church is crucial to creating an environment in the church that stimulates believers to love one another (Heb. 10:23–25). This is the most essential attribute that must dominate the life of the church. This actually models the level of commitment that believers have for Christ (Matt. 22:37–40; John 13:34–35).

Beloved, let us love one another, for love is from God; and everyone who loves is born of God and knows God. The one who does not love does not know God; for love is from God; and everyone who loves is born of God and knows God. The one who does not love does not know God, for God is love. By this the love of God was manifested in us, that God has sent His only begotten Son into the world so that we might live through Him. In this is love, not that we loved God, but that He loved us and sent His Son to be the propitiation for our sins. Beloved, if God so loved us, and His love is perfected in us. By this we know that we abide in Him and He in us, because He has given us of His spirit (1 John 4:7–13).

As they use their gift, the Holy Spirit fits the body together fitly so that the body of Christ is built up (Eph. 4:12,16). This creates unity (Eph. 4:13), which is the very thing that Christ prayed for (John 17:20–22) and gave spiritual gifts to achieve (1 Cor. 12:4–7; Eph. 4:1–8). The result? Each believer is perfected in Christ (John 17:23). Perfecting believers is one of the primary reasons the church was established.

> We proclaim Him, admonishing every man and teacher every man with all wisdom, so that we may present every man complete in Christ. For this purpose also I labor, striving according to His power, which mightily works within me (Col. 1:28–29).

Without vision, the people perish (Prov. 29:18). They go from Sunday to Sunday with no direction and they soon become despondent and begin coming to church here and there. The community suffers because the church becomes a praise rally and a Bible class. As one famous preacher says, it becomes a big huddle, forgetting that the only purpose for a huddle in the football game is to put a plan together to do something at the line of scrimmage.

### Ministry Function

The ministry's function is designed to allow the pastor to care for God's flock with decency and order, and visit those who are ill or grieving. It develops leaders so that they function as true disciples of Jesus Christ. It is designed to prepare leaders to serve as prayer warriors for the entire church. It keeps up with every member so that if they were missing they would be contacted. Whatever this ministry organizes, it does so in order that every member of the church is impacted so that God's flock is strengthened to do work of service. This ministry services as a support to all the other ministries of the church. It serves to assist the pastor as he seeks.

## THE BIBLICAL PHILOSOPHY OF THE FELLOWSHIP MINISTRY

### Definition of Fellowship

Fellowship (*koinonia*) means companionship or partnership and communion with others on the basis of something held in common (Acts 2:44).

### Biblical Philosophy of Fellowship

Fellowship is designed to promote the interpersonal caring and sharing of God's people one to another as an outgrowth of our fellowship with God (Matt. 22:37–40; Acts 2:42).

### What is True Fellowship?

- Genuine fellowship only takes place when believers are growing spiritually. It is as a result of a growing relationship with Christ that relationships with other believers become meaningful.

- Believers must be focused on the need for fellowship to fulfill their commitment to God (Eph. 4:12–13). Their focus in the local church is:

  » to edify each other to maturity (Matt. 28:19–20; Col. 1:28).

  » to evangelize in the community (Acts 1:8).

  » to work toward unity (Eph. 2:16–18; Rom. 14:19; 12:18; Heb. 12:14; 2 Tim. 2:22).

  » to encourage one another in word and deed (Col. 3:17).

  » to be salt and light in the community (Matt. 5:13–16).

  » to love (John 13:35). Believers are compelled to love as Christ loved (Eph. 5;2). Sincere relationships in the church body are a manifestation of true spiritual growth.

- Believers need to have a proper view of each other as set forth by God's Word (Phil. 2:1–5; Eph. 4:29–32; 5:4).

- Believers must seek to settle their differences in a manner that will glorify Christ (Matt. 18:15–20; 2 Cor. 2:5–13; Rom. 14–15).

### How Fellowship Occurs in the Church

- Communion or fellowship together at the Lord's Supper (1 Cor. 10:16–21; 11:23–26).

- Enjoy fellowship through corporate worship (Heb. 10:24–25; Mal. 3:16; Acts 2:42).

- Fellowship in suffering (Phil. 3:10; Col. 1:24).

- Ministering to the needs of the saints (Heb. 13:16; Rom. 15:26; 1 John 3:16–19; Jas. 2:14–16).

- Fellowship activities that will encourage individuals to meet others outside the circles they have grown accustomed to.

### *Summary*

Worship is an act of devotion to God that matures as the believer matures. Anyone who is growing spiritually will begin to imitate the character of Christ, which will result in a demonstration of His love (John 13:34–35; 1 John 4:7–12). Love magnifies itself in the life of the believer as the believer functions in the life of the church. This process produces genuine relationships, which leads to true fellowship.

## THE BIBLICAL PHILOSOPHY OF THE WORSHIP MINISTRY

Worship in the Old Testament was God's way of purifying Abraham's descendants who left Egypt for the Promised Land. He wanted them to be holy as He is holy (Lev. 11:44–45; 19:2; 20:7). Worship, which means "to bow down" or "prostrate oneself" (Gen. 22:5; 42:6; 48:12; Exod. 24:1; Jud. 7:15), was characterized by works of service performed at the temple through the offerings brought by the Israelites. The consistency of these offerings proved faithfulness to God's commands, and commitment to nurture a relationship with Him. There were five major offerings—the Burnt, Meal, Peace, Sin and Trespass Offerings—and an atonement offering for the unknown sins of all the Israelites. The Sin Offering spoke of sin as mankind's nature; whereas, the Trespass Offering was for sin as an act against God.

The process functioned this way. First when someone committed a sin they brought a Trespass Offering and they received forgiveness. Next, they would offer a Sin Offering to expiate guilt; a Peace Offering to renew their relationship with God; a Meal Offering as an expression of gratitude for God's faithfulness and grace; and finally a Burnt Offering, which was an act of utter devotion to the will of God and craving for God's complete ownership.

In the New Testament, the people gathered at the temple for worship (Acts 2:46; 3:1; 5:20, 42). However, they began to turn to private residences (Acts 2:46; 5:42; 12:12), and instead of making animal sacrifices they celebrated the Lord's Supper, which memorialized the sacrificial death of Christ. The Lord's Supper was later celebrated as the Lord's Day, and became a regular form of Christian worship (John 20:19, 26; Acts 20:7; 1 Cor. 16:2; Rev. 1:10).

Preaching and teaching became elements of supreme importance because believers needed to be taught about this "new way" (Acts 11:26; 15:35; 18:25; 20:7). The meetings ultimately included prayer (Acts 2:42; 1 Cor. 14:14–16), singing (Eph. 5:19; Col. 3:16), and giving to help those in need (2 Cor. 9:6–15;1 Cor. 16:1–3). Jesus Christ did not specifically outline an order of worship; He only provided us what needed to take place in worship. He did say that we should worship Him in "spirit and in truth" (John 4:23), and cautioned that true worship goes beyond mere outward forms (Matt. 6:1–18).

The Apostle Paul in the book of Acts provides us guidelines of how worship should function in the New Testament Church (Acts 2:42–47; 1 Cor. 11:14; 1 Tim. 2:15). In the New Testament, even though our sacrifice is permanent (Christ Jesus) and the offerings are no longer necessary (Eph. 2:15), the principles that once guided these offerings still manifest themselves in the life of the New Testament Church. It occurs in this way:

> When we first come, as awakened and believing sinners to the cross, the first thing we see in it is forgiveness of our many *trespasses*. But scarcely have we begun to rejoice in the forgiveness of our sins before we realize that there is a further and deeper need, namely, sin in our nature. This further need is met by a deeper insight into the meaning of the cross. Christ not only died for our sins; He bore our sin, as typified in the *Sin offering*. It is then, when we realize that both sins and sin have been dealt with in the cross that we enter into wonderful peace with God, as set forth in the *Peace Offering*. Then, still further, we find rest and joy and complete acceptance with God in the glorious perfection of Christ as typified in the *Meal Offering*; while more and more we come into fellowship with God through the fullness of that one perfect offering to God on our behalf this is set forth in the *Burnt Offering*.[1]

---

1. J. Sidlow Baxter, *Explore the Book*, I (Grand Rapids: Zondervan, 1987), 124–125.

God's focus remains the same. We must "be holy as He is Holy," (1 Pet. 1:16), and to be totally committed to Him (Rom. 12:1–2).

Worship has as its primary goal to provide meaningful adoration and praise to God through Jesus Christ. This is done through songs and hymns, singing praises, and spiritual songs to God. Worship must include the preaching and teaching of God's Word, prayer, giving, the fellowship of believers who stimulate each other to love and good deeds, and to administer the ordinances (Heb. 10:23–25). Each believer must be challenged to no longer concentrate on self, but focus on the power, faithfulness and glory of God (Col. 3:15–17). They must celebrate His nature in spirit and in truth (John 4:24).

### Purpose of Worship

The purpose of worship is to give expression to a relationship that has been established by God, as a result of the believer's stated belief in Christ's atonement, death and resurrection. It is practiced as a result of believers giving homage to God in thought, feeling and action, with or without the aid of symbols and rites. "Therefore, since we receive a kingdom which cannot be shaken, let us show gratitude, by which we may offer to God an acceptable service with reverence and awe; for our God is a consuming fire" (Heb. 12:28–29). The object of worship is for the believer to become fully engulfed in all that the Trinity means as represented in, and through the life and ministry of the believer (Luke 17:21; Eph. 1:3,20; 2:6; 3:11).

### Biblical Description of Worship

Worship, in the verb form, means the paying of homage or respect. The term is also used to refer to reverent devotion, service, or honor, whether public or individual, paid to God. It is the adoration, veneration, exaltation, and magnification of God. It is when we respect, esteem, love and admire God that we are worshipping Him. Worship is totally concerned with the worthiness of God, not the worthiness of the worshipper (Judson Cornwall).

Worship cannot occur without total commitment (Rom. 12:1) to a personal day-to-day walk with Christ (Matt. 4:10; Eph. 4:1–3; 5:2). It involves time, commitment, prayer, the Lord's Supper and fellowship (Acts 2:42), thanksgiving, praise, and the reading and teaching of scripture (Col. 3:15–17; 1 Tim. 4:11–16). Worship must also be an expression of a walk of faith with Christ through giving (Prov. 11:24–25; 2 Cor. 9:6–15). Giving magnifies a worshipful committed relationship with Christ (2 Cor. 9:12–15; 1 Cor. 16:1–2; 1 Tim. 6:18). It needs to be our first fruits, not our "leftovers" because this angers God (Mal. 3).

Worship should also be a time of thanksgiving to God for His goodness, faithfulness and grace. Psalm 95 is an excellent illustration. It is composed of two parts, first, a call to praise the Lord of all the earth (vss. 1–5); second, a call to acknowledge through a submissive attitude and obedient heart, the Lord's kingship over His people (vss. 6–11). The total focus of the worship service is to focus on thanksgiving and praise, not a request for needs (Ps. 29:2; Ps. 96:9; Ps. 138:2).

### Object of Worship

But the hour cometh, and now is, when the true worshippers shall worship the Father in spirit and in truth; for the Father seeketh such to worship him. God is a Spirit: and they that worship Him must worship Him in spirit and in truth (John 4:23–24).

The object of worship is to worship God through Christ, as a result of Christ's death and resurrection in spirit and truth.

When a believer experiences this fellowship and unity in the body, the full benefit of belonging to Christ remains fresh (Heb. 10:19–20; Ps. 100), so that the fruit of the Spirit grows continuously and each believer experiences their fullest potential (Gal. 5:22–23).

### Basis of Worship

- God is the one who sustains us physically and spiritually. Mankind is totally dependent upon Him like a fish is dependent upon water (Ps. 146:6–9).

- He is not just the Maker and Sustainer of heaven and earth; He will also reign over it forever (Ps. 146:10).

- He forgives us for all of our sins, permanently (Heb. 7:24,27; Rom. 8:39) and continuously (1 John 1:9).

- He will care for us every day as Christ stands as our permanent mediator between God and man (Heb. 4:14–16; 8:6).

- He is the one who can protect us from the attacks of Satan (Eph. 6:1–18; 1 John 4:4).

- We are a holy priesthood that belongs to God (1 Pet. 2:9). We are no longer our own (1 Cor. 6:19–20; 7:23; Rom. 6:22; Col. 3:3).

- Jesus Christ serves as the chief cornerstone for our new life in Him (Eph. 2:20; John 14:6; 15:5).

- Power for life is received as a result of worship (Acts 16:25–35).

### How Should We Worship?

- We should worship corporately (Ps. 34:1–3; Heb. 10:25) and individually (Pss. 23, 25, 26 et. al.).

- We should praise His goodness as well as His attributes (Ps. 46).

- We should worship through Psalms (recalling His wonderful acts), hymns (give praise for who He is), and spiritual songs (songs of encouragement to each other, Col. 3:15–17).

- We should first honor Him with our lives or He rejects our singing and offerings (Amos 5; Malachi 2:13–16; Matt. 5:21–26).

- We should give praise and glory to His name (Neh. 9:5; Rom. 10:13).

- We should worship Him in total adoration and awe (Rev. 11:16; Heb. 12:28–29).

### Examples of Worship

- Luke 1:46–55

- Luke 2:13–14

- Matthew 2:10–12

- Revelation 4:8

- Revelation 4:11

- Revelation 5:9–12

### *Summary*

Worship is an act of devotion to God that matures as the believer matures. Anyone who is growing spiritually will begin to imitate the character of Christ, which will result in a demonstration of His love in and through the believer. This love magnifies itself in the life of the believer as the believer functions in the life of the church.

## THE BIBLICAL PHILOSOPHY
## OF THE DISCIPLESHIP MINISTRY

### *Introduction*

Christ's commission to His leaders was to do two things; evangelize and make disciples. Christ stated that a disciple is someone who is made through the teaching and the observation of those who model the teaching. This means that discipleship at its core promotes the teaching of the inerrant Word of God while fostering a willing response of personal obedience to the Word of God through accountable relationships.

Discipleship does not occur overnight. It takes time. It occurs as a result of relationships developed over time that impact the heart of the follower. When the love for Christ dominates the life of a believer, the believer's commitment to Christ will lead to a deeper commitment to the church and its leadership. Leaders must be committed to this process or the membership will become ineffective (2 Cor. 3:5–6). Attending Bible study, giving to the church, being involved in worship, serving the needs of the members of the church, will all become a burden—a problem rather than their passion. Because a true disciple is not only someone who is faithful to the Lord, they are also empowered by God (Col. 1:29). This is the goal of discipleship. The process blesses the life of the believer and promotes the kingdom agenda of God.

### A Definition of Discipleship

Discipleship is that process of spiritual development which occurs in the framework of the accountable relationships of the local church whereby Christians are progressively brought from spiritual infancy to spiritual maturity and are to repeat the process with others (Dr. Tony Evans).

### Biblical Characteristic of a True Disciple

A learner, pupil and follower; someone whose whole life, as a result of a calling, has been redirected to total obedience to the caller (John 14:15; 2 Tim. 2;2; 1 John 2:3–6).

- Has the mind of Christ (Rom. 12:2; Phil. 2:5). They set their mind on the things of the Spirit rather than things of the flesh (Rom. 8:5–17).

- Loves other believers (John 13:35).

- Willing to obey God's Word (John 8:31) because of his or her love for God (John 14:15).

- Trustworthy and reliable (1 Cor. 4:2).

- Teachable (2 Tim. 2:15).

- Willing to teach others (2 Tim. 2:2).

- Views service for Christ as a privilege rather than a chore (Phil. 3:7–16).

- Views their life in the world of less importance than their life in Christ (John 12:23–26; Luke 14:25–27).

- Loves God so much they end up loving their lives less (Matt. 10:39).

- Shows a dependence on the work of the Holy Spirit in their lives (Rom. 8:11).

- Consistently demonstrates the fruit of the Spirit (John 15:5; Matt. 7:20; Col. 1:10).

### Summary Philosophy Statement for Discipleship

This ministry is designed to shape a believer from infancy to maturity. It is designed to teach believers the truth, and by lifestyle models, encourage them to consistently apply God's Word to life issues. It is this ministry's goal to present each believer complete in Christ so that the agenda of God manifests itself in the life of the believer and in the health and strength of the church.

### Summary

Whether it is leadership training, marriage counseling, AWANA, Youth Ministry, Young Adult Ministry, Singles Ministry, Men's Ministry, Life Application classes, Center for Christian Learning, Tuesday Bible Study, Women's Ministry, or Sunday worship, the purpose is to help every person who joins the church to be complete in Christ. "We proclaim Him, admonishing every man and teaching every man with all wisdom, so that we may present every man complete in Christ" (Col. 1:28).

## BIBLICAL PHILOSOPHY
## FOR THE CHILDREN AND YOUTH MINISTRY

### Overview

The Children and Youth Ministry was established with the commitment to teach both children and youth to love God with "all their hearts souls and minds, and to love their neighbor as themselves" (Matt. 22:37–40). This developmental process takes place as a result of training teachers to effectively nurture the lives of children and youth. The purpose is to teach children and youth to love the Word of God so that it becomes something they are excited about living and sharing. It is to encourage them to serve so that being a part of the Lord's ministry is an active experience.

Assisting parents in developing their children is extremely important because it establishes the life of Christ in the life of a child or youth. This is best way to instill principles that can guard their lives (Prov. 3; 6:20–23).

But Jesus said, "Let the children alone, and do not hinder them from coming to Me; for the kingdom of heaven belongs to such as these." (Matt. 19:14–15).

Remember also your Creator in the days of your youth, before the evil days come and the years draw near when you will say, "I have no delight in them" (Eccles. 12:1–2).

This process of nurturing children and youth is then extended to the community so that they come to a saving knowledge of Jesus Christ. These saved children and youth are then challenged to give their heart, soul and mind to the Lord Jesus Christ forever through a discipleship process.

### *Children's Ministry Overview*

The Children's Ministry (zero to twelve years old) is not a babysitting service; it is designed to minister in a relevant manner to the children and to also encourage parents to participate in the worship service or Bible study without distraction. Children will be taught through play and by using materials that maintain the child's attention. There are several different ministry efforts that are in place to disciple the child to spiritual maturity: teacher training, AWANA (Approved Workmen Are Not Ashamed) Club, Tuesday Night Bible Study, children's worship, Life Application classes, Vacation Bible School, KAA (Kids Across America) camp, and the Puppet Ministry.

### *Our Goal*

Our goal is to communicate God's Word by song, play and/or message, and to enable the children to take "brain knowledge" and make it a "foot work." As we work as a team (parent+child+teachers), we hope to develop a deep sense of love and respect for our Lord Jesus Christ in the mind and heart of the child, so that what is taught in the home can be reinforced at church, and what is taught at church is nurtured to maturity in the home.

### *Objectives*

- Provide training for all teachers.

- Research materials and lesson plans that will keep the children's attention.

- Develop effective teaching methods.

- Develop a well-structured exciting Sunday worship ministry.

- Continue to establish the Puppet Ministry and incorporate youth participation.

- Evangelize children in the community.

- Help each child learn memory verses each Sunday.

- Help each child to learn and know the books of the Bible in the proper order.

- Help the child learn various aspects of the Bible and the main stories, especially the birth of Christ.

- Help the child learn specific biblical principles that are significant for Christian living.

- Keep each child motivated to learn.

### Youth Vision Statement

"The vision of this youth ministry is to reach youth with a strong dynamic ministry that will impact youth to stand for Christ. We feel that this impact would involve discipling youth to reach a level of spiritual growth that wherever they go they will be able to show by example their commitment to Christ and be a witness to other youth who don't know Christ. This ministry will seek to equip, and establish its youth through education (The Word of God), Fellowship and Activities, Outreach and Evangelism."

### Youth Ministry Objectives

- Challenge teens to develop a growing relationship with Jesus Christ.

- Develop a strong administration team so that the youth ministry functions decently and in order.

- Consistently work out the theme of the youth ministry to make sure the vision of the youth ministry ties to the church's vision.

- Identify gifts and talents and encourage youth to use them in different parts of the ministry.

- Have one youth retreat at least once every two years.

- Have an effective outreach program, at least four events per year.

- Develop a youth evangelistic team.

- Develop a Parent Advisory Group that may serve as a support mechanism for the ministry.

- Hold regular monthly fellowship activities.

- Develop a youth ministry newsletter

- Develop a "Student of the Month" program as a reward system to encourage youth.

- Develop a Sports Ministry that in three years will be fully functional in the church and community.

- Fully develop the youth music team and drama team. This team can help with outreach programs like going into parks to reach young people for Christ.

- Sponsor a city-wide youth rally along with partnership churches in the area.

### *Youth Ministry Philosophy*

There are five important ingredients that should characterize the youth ministry:

1. Bible studies that minister to the diverse needs of the youth.

2.  A functional, biblically-based approach to youth programs and activities with the fostering of genuine relationships among the young people.

3.  Discipling of youth leaders so that they in turn disciple other young people.

4.  Well-structured ministries allowing for progressive spiritual growth among youth.

5.  Challenging youth to participate in evangelism and numerous outreach efforts.

### *Elements of an Effective Youth Ministry*

- Biblical foundation that determines the nature of the ministry.

- Well-organized activities that stimulate the young people to grow spiritually, make friends and have fun.

- Educational program for teaching youth in an effective manner.

- Relevant worship that is sensitive to the world that youth live in each day, while maintaining the church's biblical principles and philosophy.

- Encouragement to share their faith.

- Clear, measurable goals and objectives.

### *Biblical Philosophy for Youth Ministry*

- The Youth Ministry is controlled and shaped by the authority of God's inerrant Word:

    » All truth is God's truth. It is this truth that matures and empowers each youth.

» God's Word should be taught in a manner that would stimulate youth to live it.

» God's life-changing Word is not an alternative; it is the standard for Christian living. Even though it is the standard for all living, it is essential that the young people see God's Word as relevant for all areas of their lives.

- The youth philosophy must rest on an accurate view of God:

  » God has a personal interest in them.

  » God is gracious, sovereign, holy and just.

  » Our God is the same (but still practical for Christian living today) yesterday, today and forever. As a result, God is the most stable power they can continually experience.

- The youth philosophy must rest on an accurate view of man:

  » Man is sinful and 100% lost.

  » Man has value; God made man in His own image; that image was effaced but not erased in the fall of man.

  » God personally cares for man. This can be seen due to God's willingness to sacrifice His only begotten Son for man.

  » God's plan crosses all national, racial, economic and ethnic barriers.

## *Youth Ministry Objectives*

- General

  » To educate, evangelize and edify the youth so that they can grow and mature in Christ.

» To present believers complete in Christ, fully equipped for works of service (Col. 1:28–29; Eph. 4:12–13).To create an environment that encourages young people to build relationships.

- Environment

  » To create an environment that allows for a wide variety of personalities. The young people should not be made to think that they are only accepted when they "fit in."

  » To create an environment that encourages young people to build relationships.

  » To create an environment where young people know that God's Word is the standard for living.

- Specific

  » Education: To provide a means by which each young person has the freedom to practice and be held accountable to implement what he/she learned from the lessons.

  » Edification: To provide a means by which the teacher can see the young people put their faith into action.

  » Evangelism: To provide opportunities for the young people to share their faith in Christ.

  » Discipleship: To develop a discipleship training program designed to equip young people to disciple other young people.

## THE BIBLICAL PHILOSOPHY FOR OUTREACH MINISTRY

### Biblical Importance of Outreach Through the Church

The keys to the gates of Hades are in the Church (Matt. 16:10–20). All of the problems we face in our communities, country and world can find their answers through the powerful Word of God (2 Pet. 1:3–5). Christ took on Satan, died and arose. He is now the head of the Church (Eph. 1:22; Col. 1:18), and all power is in His hands (Matt. 28:18). The problems we encounter are really not the major issue today. The issue today is finding humble men and women who will live submissive lives focused on Christ, using His keys to unlock the death and decay that plague our communities.

When Christ was on earth, not only lives were changed, but whole communities were changed for the glory of God. We see the same results take place when His disciples focused on serving. The New Testament Church and the disciples were so strong and powerful that governments spent a lot of time trying to destroy them. Christ stated that we would do greater things (John 14:12–14). Have we?

Why are our communities falling apart right around us? I would like to propose that it is not because of the sinners; it is because of the righteous. 2 Chronicles 15:37; 1 Chronicles 7:14 and 1 Corinthians 5:12–13 instruct us that the problem is with the unbelieving righteous who refuse to live lives that are in total submission to God. In 2 Peter 2 and Hosea 4:6 the false preachers are accused of causing destruction and decay.

Jesus Christ came to "seek and to save those who are lost" (Luke 19:10). These individuals who are designed by God are social, physical and spiritual beings. Christ did not seek to save them without impacting them in all these areas. This is the reason Christ did not just teach the people of Israel, He fed them from five loaves and two fishes. He healed the sick and blind (Mark 6:5–6; Luke 7:1–10). Christ said; "The Spirit of the Lord is upon Me, because He anointed me to preach the Gospel to the poor. He has sent Me to proclaim release to the captives and recovery of sight to the blind, to set free those who are downtrodden, to proclaim the favorable year of the Lord" (Luke 4:18–19).

### *Biblical Definition of the New Testament Church as it Relates to the Community*

- The purpose of the church is to be a community where believers use their gifts to serve God for honor and glory (1 Pet. 4:10; Rom. 12:4–6; 1 Cor. 12:21–31).

- The church should be a viable process that impacts believer's lives, constantly stimulating spiritual and numerical growth (through teaching, praying, fellowship and evangelism: Acts 2:42–47; Col. 1:28–29) and commitment to Christ through His word (1 Tim. 4:8; 2 Tim. 3:16–17).

- The church should be an environment where the believers are constantly stimulated to submit every part of their lives to the authority of God (Rom. 12:1–2; Col. 3:16).

- The New Testament Church must demonstrate the glory of God (1 Cor. 10:31; Col. 3:15–17; Eph. 5:20).

- The Church should impact a believer so that the believer impacts society (Matt. 5:16–17; 17:18–20; Matt. 25:31–46; Jas. 2:14–17).

- The Church represents and reflects the person, program and glory of God in history (Luke 17:21; Col. 1:15–20). It is a nation unto itself (1 Pet. 2:9–10). This is why it has its own:
  » Court system (1 Cor. 6:1–11).
  » Accountability process (Matt. 18:15–18; 1 Pet. 4:17).
  » Care ministry (John 13:34–35).
  » Social service ministry (1 John 3:17; Jas. 2:14–17).
  » Social justice system (Jas. 2:1–13).

- The Church must move from programs to comprehensive ministries. It must seek to impact the whole man (Eph. 4:11–13,16; Col. 1:28).

- The Church must not be satisfied with mediocrity; it must always strive for excellence (Col. 1:16–18). When this occurs, the Church proves itself effective in the community and the world, demonstrating that the gates of hell have indeed not prevailed.

### Summary

The New Testament local church represents a group of baptized believers of Jesus Christ (1 Cor. 1:2; 12:12–14), working together to carry out His plans, purpose and will (Eph. 1:11). These believers must gather regularly (1 Cor. 1:2; 11:18; Acts 20:7; Heb. 10:24–25) for the building up and equipping of one another (Eph. 4:11–13; 1 Tim. 4:1–16) through the teaching, prayer, singing, Lord's Supper, and fellowship (Acts 2:42). This will be done as a result of the use of individual gifts (Rom. 12:3–21; 1 Cor. 12–14) so that believers will be imitators of Christ (Eph. 4:1–2; 5:1–2) to be presented perfect in Him (Col. 1:28–29). These believers must then become witnesses for Christ in the local community and the world (Acts 2:42–27; 13:1–4).

### Social Service...Community Impact
### General Principles

The urban church must emphasize sound biblical teaching (2 Tim. 4:2–3) with the focus of modeling believers who represent Christ on earth before the community and the world. This salts the community and provides light in the darkness (Matt. 5:13–15).

> But even if you should suffer for what is right, you are blessed. Do not fear what they fear; do not be frightened. But in your hearts set apart Christ as Lord. Always be prepared to give an answer to everyone who asks you to give the reason for the hope that you have. But do this with gentles and respect, keeping a clear conscience, so that those who speak maliciously against your good behavior in Christ may be ashamed of their slander (1 Pet. 3:14–16).

### Christ's View of Social Impact (outline by Dr. Tony Evans)

- Christ saw social liberation as the natural outworking of His gospel mission (Luke 4:18).

- Christ exemplified social liberation on behalf of people who paths crossed His (Mark 6:5–6; Luke 7:1–10; John 6:1–15).

- The Church is to support governmental efforts to rule society righteously (Rom. 13).

- The Church can challenge the illegal and unrighteous rule of government (Acts 16:35–40).

- The Church is to model social righteousness before the world (John 13:35; Acts 2:45).

- The Church is commanded to alleviate the social suffering of its members (1 Tim. 5:3–10; Acts 4:32–37), and resist any attempts to create social destruction among its members (Jas. 2:1–9).

Jesus says,

The Spirit of the Lord is on Me because He has anointed Me to preach good news to the poor. He has sent Me to proclaim freedom for the prisoners and recovery of sight for the blind, to release the oppressed . . . (Luke 4:18).

### *Conclusion*

When biblical principles for church development are examined and applied, they expose the express reason why Christ established the Church. Its mission is to restore people spiritually, emotionally and physically to be complete in Christ (Col. 1:28–29). This ministry is focused on influencing the community and the world by the power of God so that the rule of God is established in the community for God's glory (1 Tim. 3:15; 1 Pet. 2:9–10; 4:17).

With our communities decaying morally, and with a value system that is null and void, the Church needs more than ever to be the Church through its teaching, accountability and comprehensive approach to reach the whole man.

If the Church is not focused on God's agenda, it has usurped its power and its reason for biblical existence.

## BIBLICAL PHILOSOPHY
## FOR EVANGELISM AND MISSIONS MINISTRY

### *Biblical Importance of Evangelism and Missions*

Jesus Christ came to "seek and to save those who are lost" (Luke 19:10). This call is not just for those in the local community which the church resides in, but it is also for all those around the world (Acts 1:8). "Jesus said to them, 'My food is to do the will of Him who sent Me and to accomplish His work. Do you not say, 'There are yet four months, and then comes the harvest?' Behold, I say to you, lift up your eyes and look on the fields, that they are white for harvest. Already he who reaps is receiving wages and is gathering fruit for life eternal; so that he who sows and he who reaps may rejoice together. For in this case the saying true, 'One sows and another reaps.' I sent you to reap that for which you have not labored; others have labored and you have entered into their labor'" (John 4:34–38).

### *The Biblical and Theological Mandate for Evangelism*
### *Biblical injunctions on the need for evangelism*

- People are lost and separated from God (Matt. 9:36; Luke 19:10; Eph. 2:1,12; 2 Tim. 2:26).

- People have no desire to seek God on their own (Rom. 3:10–12).

- People are unable to save themselves (Eph. 2:8–9).

- Christ was willing to die for our sins so that man might know God (Rom. 5:8; 1 John 4:10).

- The Holy Spirit will remove the blinder from the mind of the unbeliever as a result of the presentation of the gospel (2 Cor. 4:1–7).

- God is patient (with respect to judgment) so that people may not perish, but rather repent (2 Pet. 3:9).

- People need to be told about Christ (Matt. 28:18–20; Rom. 10:14–15).

- God has given us the responsibility to be ambassadors for Christ, that people might be reconcile to God through Christ (2 Cor. 5:18–21).

- Christ's love should motivate us to obey (2 Cor. 5:14; Rom. 5:5).

- The "Evangelists" in the Epistles
  - » Acts 21:8—Philip
  - » Ephesians 4:11—part of the list
  - » 2 Timothy 4:5—Timothy

### *Theological Considerations for Evangelism*
### *Evangelism is rooted in the nature of God*

- The Father's love (Jer. 31:3; John 3:16)

- The Son's mission (John 3:16, 6:44; Heb. 1:3)

- The Spirit's mission (John 15:26–27; Acts 1:8)

- God's call to Abraham (Gen. 12:3): "all peoples on earth will be blessed through you."

### *The need for evangelism is rooted in the condition of man*

- The Bible says that man is made under the dominion of flesh, sin, law, and death. Man is depicted as depraved and dead in his sin.

- Increasingly severe crimes, even at lower age levels, teen pregnancy, homosexuality, drug abuse, etc. provide ample evidence that man is under the dominion of the flesh.

### *Evangelism was the root of Christ's focus on earth*

- Jesus came to seek and save the lost (Luke 19:10). His focus was not on the righteous but the unrighteous (Matt. 9:12–13).

- Paul: "For woe is me if I do not preach the gospel" (1 Cor. 9:16).

- Andrew: John 1:40–42

- John Knox: "Give me Scotland or I die."

### *Significant Principles for Church Evangelistic Impact to the Community and the World*

Any church that is not focused on reaching out to a lost world is missing its calling. Evangelism and missions cannot be an option in the New Testament church; it must be the standard by which the Church functions.

It is the focal point of God's love manifested through Christ (John 3:16). The Church with Christ as its head (Col. 1:18) and chief cornerstone (Eph. 2:20) therefore has no option.

### *Definition of Evangelism*

Evangelism is the proclamation of the historical, biblical Christ as Savior and Lord in the community and the world with the intent of persuading people to come to Christ personally and to be reconciled to God. This call is for persons to deny themselves, take up the cross, and identify themselves with His new community. Evangelism is *never* a message separated from the individual. It is a message that is demonstrated through the lifestyle and words of an individual (1 Tim. 4:15–16). The results of evangelism include obedience to Christ, incorporation into His Church and responsible service in the world. Evangelism should be defined not only in terms of its results but also its methods and message.

Originally the word "evangelism" meant reward for good news. It later changed to mean good news.

That is, good news that Jesus Christ died, arose and is now alive in heaven. His death is a gift of salvation for all men, both Jew and Gentile (Acts 1:8). This is the gospel (1 Cor. 15:3–8).

There are three stages in the evangelism process:

1. leading a person to Christ by explaining Jesus as the Christ, the Son of God that is God;

2. orienting the person to the essential principles of the Word;

3. discipling the person to maturity by teaching Bible doctrine and church involvement (Eph. 4:11–16).

### *Summary*

The Gospel is the power of God (1 Cor. 1:17). As an instrument of the Holy Spirit, it convicts (1 Thess. 1:5; John 16:7–9), converts and bears fruit (Col. 1:6). Although often opposed (1 Thess. 2:2), it is not itself restricted (2 Thess. 2:9). Even if its proclaimers are opposed (Philemon 13), they should proclaim it with boldness (Eph. 6:19), for to those who respond to it in faith, it is the "power of God for salvation" (Rom. 1:16). (from Rev. Michael P. Green)

## A BIBLICAL PHILOSOPHY OF ADMINISTRATION MINISTRY

### Overview

Although the scriptures say little on the subject, it is generally accepted that Jesus spent many years working as a "carpenter's son" (Matt. 13:55). He was expected to assist Joseph in making, mending and installing various things that related to that job. Many of His close associates were businessmen. He chose fishermen, who had investments in boats and fishing equipment (Mark 1:19–20). These men had to catch their products and market them. They had to employ helpers and supervise them. As a result of Jesus's intervention, Peter caught a boatload of fish and was able to leave it to his helpers (Luke 5:1–11). This is why when problems developed (Acts 6:1–6), they could immediately begin to manage the rapid expansion of the church. When the Church grew to 3,000 people (Acts 2:41) in one service, Peter and the disciples (some who were fishermen working with Peter) knew how to begin to properly administer to the needs of the church.

At the very beginning of the Church (Acts 1–6) there was no concern for the economic life or the management practice of the Church. In fact, the apostles were preoccupied with what was happening to the Gospel, i.e., what God was doing with both men and the Gospel. As the disciples increased in number, it became more difficult to maintain control when the economics and management of the local affairs were neglected. Disunity began to develop as some apparent inequities of daily distribution were voiced by some of the people. At that time the twelve disciples immediately recognized the problem area and appointed "men of good report, full of spirit and wisdom," to attend to these matters while they devoted themselves to prayer and ministry of the Word. The need for the proper organization of the church body became of extreme importance.

For a thriving Corinthian church, administration was needed and was provided as a spiritual gift (1 Cor. 12:28). As each believer used their spiritual gift for the edification of the body of Christ, this gift of administration became even more important. There was a need to make sure that the body remained organized and functional so that everything was done with decency and order (1 Cor. 14:40).

### General Principles for the Administration Ministry

The Administration Ministry is a service ministry that functions to assist other ministries fulfill their goals and objectives. Its function in the Church is not to control the development and ongoing functioning of ministries, but to service them based on the written guidelines and policies of Living Word Fellowship Church. These policies are in place to ensure that the operations of the church are done with efficiency, based on prescribed time lines. It also serves to make sure that all buildings and vehicles are secure at the end of the day and are functioning properly for the development of all ministries.

## *General Operating Principles*
### *Receipts*

General funds received are given by the body for the general operations of the church in support of the operating budget. The body specifically gives to the building fund for the construction of church facilities, and 15 percent of these funds go for building maintenance. This giving is primarily received during worship service and Tuesday Night Bible Study. A Count Team, organized by the treasurer and business manager of the church, counts the offerings. It is deposited on Monday by an armored service. General and building fund giving that is mailed or brought to the church office is to be put into the safe deposit box by the business manager, pastor's administrative assistant or the vice chairman of the elder's ministry.

Funds collected for special ministry activities are listed on the specific count sheet and deposited by the church's accounting department into the church's designated fund. These funds are miscellaneous receipts and are restricted so that they are used for their intended purposes. Funds collected for group activities are counted immediately, turned over to an elder, or the treasurer, or business manager and immediately put into the safe. Media receipts are the proceeds from the sale of tapes, CDs or DVDs. They are turned in on Sunday for the Count Team to count and list in the miscellaneous category.

Sunday giving must follow the count policy with no less than two people counting. All checks must be recorded in the church's computer system for each member's account.

### *Disbursements*

All church disbursements are to be processed based on a system for control and integrity of disbursements and timely payment of all outstanding obligations. One voucher is to be prepared per payee with supporting invoices or other documentation attached. The associate pastor responsible for that budget area must then approve the voucher. The business manager reviews all vouchers for completeness, proper account coding, and conformity to established budgets.

Non-budgeted items must be approved by the senior pastor. The assistant pastor can help by doing his best to bring this to the attention of the pastor. This includes overspending of individual account categories even if the funds are available within a particular ministry area. These non-budgeted items must be approved before the expenses are incurred.

Disbursements will be made on a weekly basis. All vouchers must be submitted to the Administration Ministry two weeks prior to the need for these funds. This ensures the funds are available when needed.

Associate pastors must make sure these procedures are followed so that members do not become frustrated and respond negatively to the administration staff. The business manager must be in constant touch with the associate pastors to ensure a smooth process.

Weekly disbursements are distributed on Wednesday mornings after the leaders have a chance to sign the checks. Emergencies that are within policy, or based on the pastor's decision, must also be approved by the assistant pastor, or the vice chairman or treasurer of the Elders Ministry.

Payroll is processed and disbursed by the 15th and 30th of each month.

Spending is monitored weekly as a result of meetings with the pastor and/or the assistant pastor.

### Financial Reporting Process

The checking account must be balanced each month and properly filed in the business office. Income statements are prepared and provided to the pastor. At the second elders' meeting each month a financial report is provided. This report must be given to the pastor, assistant pastor and treasurer one week prior to the meeting. This report provides a summary of all spending done for the prior month, and summarizes all spending to date for the year. A ledger must be provided to the treasurer. Each year, members should receive their giving reports for tax purposes.

### Summary

The Administration Ministry of the church is a ministry designed to make sure that all the church's business accounts function with decency and order. This ensures that the integrity of the leaders of the church is not damaged and the name of Christ is not maligned. It is to also keep the church activities functioning smoothly so members are not distracted from achieving ministry objectives.

You now have examples of comprehensive biblical ministry outlines designed to match vision and mission. Use these to guide your own strategic planning process. Next, evaluate the ministry structures in the Appendix and crystallize your ministry structures so that your vision to ministry strategy has form and structure. In Chapter Nine, I will provide a budget outline that fits the structure so that expenditure directly matches the vision.

## Chapter Six

# LEADERSHIP THAT MAKES A DIFFERENCE

Any leader that becomes satisfied with the "status quo" will reduce the effectiveness of the group they lead. This is because the needs of people change, so that the only consistent thing we have before us is change. Anyone who refuses to change ministry strategy and function for the sake of maintaining "status quo" soon reduces the effectiveness of the ministry to the people, and the church therefore provides little impact in the lives of people and the community. This was what Jesus experienced while He ministered on earth. The people wanted to maintain their man-made traditions and in doing so, they ignored the commands of God and rejected Christ (Matt. 15:2–6; Col. 2:6–8; John 5:39–43).

Leroy Eims in his book, *Be the Leader You Were Meant to Be*, states that there are three essential characteristics for effective/productive leadership. They are excellence, initiative, and creativity. Likewise there are three essential characteristics that will allow a leader to impact those whom he/she is leading, wholeheartedness, single-mindedness, and a fighting spirit. "The real test of your leadership is whether or not other leaders are developed as you lead the way. The development of Christlike character in the people for whom you are responsible is one of your prime objectives"[1]

---

1. LeRoy Eims, *Be the Leader You Were Meant to Be* (Colorado Springs: David C. Cook, 1996), 88.

# DEFINITION OF SPIRITUAL LEADERSHIP

We measure the effectiveness of the leader, not in terms of the leadership he exercises, but in terms of the leadership he evokes; not in terms of power over others, but in terms of the power he releases in others; not in terms of the goals he sets up and the directions he gives, but in terms of the goals and plans of action persons work out for themselves with his help; not in terms alone of products and projects completed, but in terms of growth in competence, sense of responsibility, and personal satisfactions among many participants.[2]

Spiritual leadership is the development of relationships with the people of a Christian institution or body in such a way that individuals and the group are enabled to formulate and achieve biblically compatible goals that meet real needs. By their ethical influence, spiritual leaders serve to motivate and enable others to achieve what otherwise would never be achieved.[3]

## Dimensions of Spiritual Leadership

There are three dimensions to effective church leadership:

- Personal (the individual) – care for each person in the ministry area.

- Social (the group) – work to maintain unity (unity is not everyone doing the same thing. It is everyone being faithful to carry out their responsibility focused on the same task—Philippians 2:1–2).

- Production (the job) – must be committed to achieve the prescribed goals.

## Biblical Description of the Nature of a Spiritually Empowered Leader

- Leaders must understand their gifts and commit to be good stewards of their gifts.

---

2. Grace Loucks Elliott, *How to Help Groups Make Decisions* (Seattle: CreateSpace, 2011), 43.
3. Leroy Eims, *Be the Leader You Were Meant to Be: Growing Into the Leader God Called You to Be* (Wheaton: Victor, 1975), 79.

> As each one has received a special gift, employ it in serving one another as good stewards of the manifold grace of God (1 Pet. 4:10).

> So then, men ought to regard us as servants of Christ and as those entrusted with the secret things of God. Now it is required that those who have been given a trust must prove faithful (1 Cor. 4:1–2).

- The task of a true spiritual leader is to promote growth in competence, responsibility, character, and leadership in individuals, to produce a healthy, functioning, ministering body, and to promote the achievement of the Church's goals and plans in its community (Num. 11:10–17).

- Effective, ministering churches must have leaders who:

  » can be believed and trusted.

  » put the interests of the group before personal interests (Phil. 2:4).

  » help the group define where it is going.

  » know how to get there or know how to follow through until the task is done.

  » make the mission seem important, possible and exciting.

- The leader must be willing to submit to the overall leadership structure of the church, and willing to be accountable (1 Cor. 11:3; 1 Tim. 3:4).

- An effective leader must be flexible because discovering and applying the will of God is everything (1 Cor. 16:6–7; 2 Cor. 1:15–17; Acts 16:6).

- An effective leader must be thorough (Matt. 28:19–20; Col. 1:27–28; John 17:4, 8).

- An effective leader must not run from challenges (1 Cor. 16:9; 2 Cor. 4:10).

- An effective leader has a team spirit (Eph. 4:12–16). Leaders who will excel must demonstrate the following qualities:

    » Excellence – "The spirit of excellence in the life of a leader is a reflection of one of God's attributes" (p. 8).[4]

    » Romans. 12:11—". . . not lagging, behind in diligence, fervent in spirit, serving the Lord"; also Matthew 25:14–30.

Leroy Eims says that God develops the spirit of excellence in seven ways:[5]

1. "By helping us realize our own weakness" (2 Cor. 12:9).

2. "Through the prayers of others" (Col. 4:12).

3. "Through someone sharing the Word with us" (1 Thess. 3:10).

4. "As we study for Bible for ourselves" (2 Tim. 3:16–17).

5. "Through suffering" (1 Pet. 5:10).

6. "By giving us a hunger for holiness" (2 Cor. 7:1).

7. "Through a desire to have the fruit of our lives brought to perfection" (Luke 8:14).

- A leader must take initiative:

    » "He doesn't wait for things to happen; he helps make things

---

4. Ibid., 56.
5. Ibid., 58.

happen. He's out at the point of the action. That's one reason some people shy away from leadership responsibilities."[6]

> » A leader exercises initiative by being willing to serve without anyone requesting their service. They see a need and they respond (John 13:1–17; Acts 28:2–3).

> » When there is an issue that needs to be solved between two believers, a leader takes the initiative for reconciliation to occur (Matt. 5:23–24, 18:15).

> » A leader must actively seek the information he/she needs, and must be willing to learn from others (Prov. 20:5).

> » A leader must "train himself to think ahead" (Eims). The leader must develop goals, and follow a structured process for accomplishing these goals.

- A leader must be creative:

> » "They are not afraid to try new and different things. When you look at the lives of the apostles you do not find the monotony and stiffness that characterizes so many lives today."[7]

> » "One way is to keep yourself in the proper frame of mind. Constantly be on the lookout for a better way. Train yourself to think, 'If it works, it will soon be obsolete.' Maintain an open and probing mind. Pray for the boldness and courage it will take to try something new when God reveals it to you."[8]

- A leader must provide wholehearted service to God:

---

6. LeRoy Eims, *Be the Leader You Were Meant to Be: Lessons On Leadership from the Bible* (Colorado Springs: David C. Cook, 2012), 81.
7. Ibid., 87.
8. Leroy Eims, *Be the Leader You Were Meant to Be: Growing Into the Leader God Called You to Be* (Wheaton: Victor, 1975), 67.

» "Almost daily we hear people telling us, 'Take it easy'/Don't work too hard'/'Don't overdo it.' The dangerous thing is that this lack of wholeheartedness can be picked up by the Christian leader. When it is, it spells mediocrity and failure in his work."[9]

» "Wholeheartedness and zeal are the outgrowths of a love that burns in the leader's heart. From there it spreads to the hearts and lives of others, who catch the flame of that spirit."[10]

» The model of wholehearted service to God is provided by many great leaders in God's Word (2 Chron. 31:21; Col. 3:23; Eccles. 9:10).

- A leader must be single-minded:

  » "Two things transcend this world and will last through eternity: the Word of God and people's souls. When leaders give themselves to these, they are locked on eternal values. The things of the world clamor for their attention, but he keeps his eyes single to the things that last."[11]

  » The second reason why a leader should be single-minded: "Life is too short to be wasted"; Ephesians 5:16).[12]

  » The third reason why a leader should be single-minded: his/her labor "is not in vain in the Lord" (1 Cor. 15:58).

  » The Apostle Paul said, "I press toward the mark." He did not say, "I float toward the mark; I glide toward the mark; I slip and slide

9. Ibid., 70.
10. LeRoy Eims, *Be the Leader You Were Meant to Be: Lessons On Leadership from the Bible* (Colorado Springs: David C. Cook, 2012), 98.
11. Leroy Eims, *Be the Leader You Were Meant to Be: Growing Into the Leader God Called You to Be* (Wheaton: Victor, 1975), 73.
12. Ibid., 74.

toward the mark; or I drift toward the mark." He said "press," and that always presupposes opposition (Col. 1:29).

> » Today the Lord is looking for people who care nothing for the empty praise or temporal pleasures of this world (Heb. 11:24–29). He is seeking men and women who care that the world needs Christ and who are eager to follow Him with single-mindedness and purpose.

> » "However, I consider my life worth nothing to me; my only aim is to finish the race and complete the task the Lord Jesus has given me—the task of testifying to the good news of God's grace" (Acts 20:24).

- A leader must have a fighting spirit:

  > » "But the leader must never stop there. It is not a brilliant mind but a fighting spirit that will keep him going when all semblance of order has crumbled around him."[13]

  > » 2 Chronicles 30:10 & 31:20, 1 Corinthians 9:25–27, and 2 Corinthians 11:24–28 provide some clear Bible models of a fighting spirit.

  > » "These three things, then, are essential to making an impact as a leader. We must be wholehearted, single-minded, and have a fighting spirit. Programs may continue without these, but the leader whose life is to be used of God to produce much lasting fruit will see that he has all three."[14]

- A leader must know what it takes to make that particular ministry work. A leader must exhibit faith that God will provide the workers. At the same time, they must not wait for workers to show up, but instead recruit them based on the prescribed qualifications and

---

13. Ibid., 80.
14. Ibid., 81.

responsibilities. They must approach obstacles as opportunities to experience the powerful, life-changing work of God, exhibiting the mind of an overcomer (Phil. 4:13).

> For I consider that the sufferings of this present time are not worthy to be compared with the glory that is to be revealed to us (Rom. 8:18).

> Now faith is the assurance of things hoped for, the conviction of things not seen (Heb. 11:1).

> And without faith it is impossible to please Him, for he who comes to God must believe that He is and that He is a rewarder of those who seek Him (Heb. 11:6–7).

## *Resolving Difficulties and Surviving Dangers*

- One of the keys to resolving difficulties is to first seek to be involved with the people, always demonstrating a servant attitude, allowing them to be involved in the development of that particular ministry.

> Asking people's advice and letting them in on decisions is very helpful in many ways. For one thing, the leader usually needs all the help he can get. Second, the people know they are in on the action and are making real contributions. This keeps morale high and misunderstandings to a minimum. This is a task the leader can't duck. He must face the responsibility of keeping information flowing and the lines of communication open. Though it's hard work and sometimes a pain in the neck, he'll be glad he did.[15]

- A leader must communicate with everyone that is involved with that particular ministry area. "Moses ran into this problem: 'For he supposed his brothers would have understood'" (Acts 7:25). But they didn't.

---

15. LeRoy Eims, *Be the Leader You Were Meant to Be: Lessons On Leadership from the Bible* (Colorado Springs: David C. Cook, 2012), 151.

- The leader must deal with problems right away in a loving and biblical manner. Doing it biblically keeps the process objective.

- The leader must follow the leadership system provided for the church, and not create their own order (1 Tim. 3:15).

- The leader must be honest, fair, and function with integrity (1 Tim. 4:12).

- In the midst of a conflict, a leader should not function in a quarrelsome manner (1 Tim. 6:3–5; 2 Tim. 2:14,24–26).

- A leader must be a peacemaker (Matt. 5:9; Rom. 14:19; Jas. 3:18), not by trying to make everyone happy or cause everyone to like them (Paul speaks out against this in Galatians 1:10), but by seeking to bring everyone under the authority of God's Word focused on achieving ministry objectives.

When a leader is resolving a problem, they must always remember that if the problem remains unresolved, or it ends in a negative manner, this only provides Satan an opportunity to gain a foothold (Eph. 6:12).

The greatest danger that the church faces is for leaders not to use their keys (the Word of God and prayer) when the "gates of Hades" are before them (Matt. 16:18–20).

The greatest power for overcoming all problems and surviving dangers, which also determines the nature of the persons involved in the conflict, is love (1 Cor. 13:1–8; 13). Remember "Love never fails" (1 Cor. 13:8). Christ says that we will know His disciples "if you have love for one another" (John 13:34–35). The focus of the church is to make disciples (Matt. 28:19–20; Col. 1:28–29).

If we survive dangers, we must be sure that we are not serving ourselves (Mark 12:38–40; Acts 14:14–15; 1 Thess. 2:6), because Christ says that the proud person is His enemy (1 Pet. 5:5).

The Bible states that when we resolve a problem, we have gained a brother (Matt. 18:15).

## CONCLUSION

In order for a church to continue to embody the personality of Christ and the ministry of the Holy Spirit, these principles of leadership must remain as the standard. These standards may be challenging, but once applied, they will bless the leader and everyone around them. I pray that we will allow these principles to guide the strategy of each church so that lives are changed, God's kingdom agenda for the church progresses and each member functions as salt and light to the world (Matt. 5:13–16).

# SELECTING LEADERS TO SHAPE THE VISION

As the pastor develops the ministry vision, they may find the need for new leaders. The Bible has a lot to say in this area. When Christ came, He had to select leaders. When Paul started planting churches, he had to select leaders. Moses was faced with the same dilemma as well as Samuel, Elijah and many others. Sometimes, it is not just the selection of leaders that is crucial, it is the retraining of the present leaders. You cannot teach every old dog new tricks, but you can at least teach them to bark at the real enemy, Satan.

Voting should not be a part of the selection process. This creates a political system that is based on who is popular or who has a long history at the church. The selection process should be based on criteria that Christ put in place for the development of his body, the Church. Every time leaders were selected in the Bible, from the time of Moses, it was always based on the criteria that God put in place.

"Furthermore, you shall select out of all the people able men who fear God, men of truth, those who hate dishonest gain; and you shall place these over them as elders of thousands, of hundreds, of fifties and of tens. Let them judge the people at all time; and let it be that every major dispute they will bring to you, but every minor dispute they themselves will judge. So it will be easier for you, and they will bear the burden with you. If you do this thing and God so commands you, then you will be able to endure, and all these people also will go to their place in peace" (Exod. 18:21–23).

The same is found in 1 Timothy and Titus. The only example we have of people voting for leadership is in the case of the disciple casting lots to replace Judas with Matthias (Acts 1:21–26). In this case, even though they picked Matthias, later Christ chose Paul (Acts 9). In Titus 1:5, Titus is told to select the leaders; he was not told to vote for leaders. In Acts 6, the people were told to recommend to the apostles, men who could be used as deacons. Again, criteria were provided to the people and their recommendations were determined by the apostles. "Therefore, brethren, select from among you seven men good reputation, full of the Spirit and of wisdom, who we may put in charge of this task" (Acts 6:3).

This chapter seeks to provide some biblical guidelines for how the process of selecting leaders can work. This is essential for the effective development and expansion of God's vision for the church.

## THE LEADERSHIP SELECTION PROCESS

### *Introduction*

A strong team of leaders is significant to the health and strength of the church body. The church will be as strong or as weak as its leadership team. Selecting who will enter a leadership training process must be met with prayer and even fasting (Acts 14:23). The pastor and other leaders must seek God with an open heart because the Spirit of God must guide the process through God's Word, for God's glory.

This process must never be guided by politics or personality. It must always be a process that honors God, one that falls within the guidelines of his Word and seasoned with prayer.

The kind of thoughts that must lead this process should be; "How has God equipped this individual to effectively serve, based on God's guidelines, in a leadership capacity of the church?" "One of the prime goals of a Christian leader should be the deepening of the spiritual life of the people he leads. They must grow in grace and in the knowledge of Christ, developing in their effectiveness for him and deepening in their devotion. It is God's desire that they demonstrate Christlike qualities in everyday life."[1]

---

1.  LeRoy Eims, *Be the Leader You Were Meant to Be: Lessons On Leadership from the Bible* (Colorado Springs: David C. Cook, 2012), 179.

### General Leadership Qualities

- A heart for that particular area. A leader that has a passion for a particular ministry influences others to provide energetic service which becomes contagious to other members in the church.

- A teachable spirit (2 Tim. 2:2).

- A willingness to serve others.

- A commitment to see the various tasks to completion.

- Respect for leadership and willingness to submit when there is disagreement.

### Indentifying and Choosing Potential Church Leaders
### Elders or Associate Pastors

- Must attend church on a regular basis (Heb. 10:25ff).

- He must contribute financially to the ministry of the church (1 Cor. 16:1–4;  2 Cor. 8:1–15).

- Must use his spiritual gift to actively serve in a specific ministry area (1 Cor. 12:13ff).

- Must have a good reputation among the church members (1 Tim. 3:7).

- Must participate in active service to the church at least two years prior to filling the office of elder (1 Tim. 3:6).

- Must be able to demonstrate the ability to follow the leadership of the church (1 Pet. 2:13–21).

- Must demonstrate the ability to teach and lead others (1 Tim. 2:1–3).

*Elders' Wives or Associate Pastors' Wives*

- Must have respect of others.

- Must be able to avoid repeating evil gossip.

- Must have self-control.

- Must be trustworthy in everything.

- Must fulfill the requirements outlined in (1 Tim. 3:11; 5:4–10).

- Must participate in active service to the church for at least one year.

- Must show reasonable progress in the church discipleship process.

- Must have a teachable spirit.

- Must show an attitude of humility while she is serving.

- Must be able to submit to spiritual leadership.

- Must have time to perform the assigned duties.

*Deacons*

- Worthy of respect (1 Tim. 3:9). He must speak the truth consistently.

- Not addicted to wine (1 Tim. 3:9). He is never to be controlled by alcohol.

- Not found of sordid gain (1 Tim. 3:8). Not dishonest or greedy in business.

- Tested, and must have proven record of service and personal integrity (1 Tim. 3:10).

- Husband of one wife (1 Tim. 3:12) and must be faithful to his wife morally (1 Tim. 3:2; Titus 1:7).

- Submits to spiritual leadership (Heb. 13:17).

- Manages his own household well (1 Tim. 3:12) and leads his family in the process of spiritual grown in a well-ordered manner.

- Participates in active service to the church for at least one year.

- Displays a servant attitude (Acts 6:1–6).

### Deacon's Wives

- Has the respect of others (1 Tim. 5:10).

- Avoids gossip (1 Tim. 3:11).

- Exhibits self control (1 Tim. 2:15).

- Trustworthy in everything (1 Tim. 3:11).

- Participates in active service to the church for at least one year.

- Submit to spiritual leadership (Heb. 13:17).

- Possesses a teachable spirit.

- Has time to perform the assigned duties.

### Ministers or Ministry Leaders

- Manages his home well (1 Tim. 3:4–5; 5:8). This involves the following issues:

  » His relationship with his wife and children (Eph. 5:22–6:4).

» Good financial management.

» Consistent provision of spiritual guidance for their family (Gen. 18:19).

» Reliable and teachable (1 Tim. 2:2).

» Not a recent convert (1 Tim. 3:6).

» Spiritual-minded (Acts 6:3; Exodus 18:19–23; Deut. 1:13–15).

» Committed to love other believers (John 13:35).

» Committed to developing a unified body of believers (John 17:20–23).

» Not divisive (Rom. 16:17–18; Titus 3:9–11).

» Committed to discipleship (Matt. 28:19–20; Luke 14:26–33; Col. 1:28–29), and to disciplining others (1 Tim. 2:2).

» Demonstrated fidelity to God's Word (John 8:31; 14:15; 1 John 2:3–6).

» Consistent attendance and interest in Bible study, Sunday School and worship (Rom. 12:2; Phil. 2:5).

» Demonstrated dependence on the work of the Holy Spirit in their lives (Rom. 8:9–11).

» Not argumentative (1 Tim. 6:3–5; 1 Tim. 2:14, 24; Prov. 17:19).

» Demonstrates the fruit of the Spirit in their lives (Galatians 5:22–26).

» Committed to financially supporting the church (Luke 6:38, Matt. 6:19–24).

## *Process for Choosing Potential Leaders*
### *Process for the nomination of elders*
#### Selection

Prior to the annual church business meeting, nominations for men to be considered for the office of elder shall be selected by the elders. Their names will be submitted to the congregation. The congregation will be requested to review the names. If any member of the congregation has questions or objections to the selected individual(s) then the elders will meet to entertain the concerns to see whether or not they are valid. If the concerns are not valid, the Elder's Ministry will interview the elders and their wives. Upon the review of the interview(s), the elders will decide whether to place the person in training or to remove the person(s) from further consideration.

#### Approval

The Elder's Ministry shall have the responsibility to assess the qualifications for each prospective candidate to determine eligibility.

#### Training

Each candidate, upon approval, shall be placed in a training program for an unspecified period of time. The Elder's Ministry shall oversee and administer this training program.

### *Ordination of elders*

Each elder shall be ordained after successfully completing a year of supervised ministry training under the direction to the Elder's Ministry. After it is determined that the elder (based on a final interview and vote of elders) in training has met all the spiritual and personal qualifications, an ordination service shall be conducted. At this service, the elder shall be presented for congregational affirmation. The elder shall receive the "laying on of hands" by the Elder's Ministry signifying his acceptance and approval by the church.

#### Approval

Upon verification of completion of the training program, each nominee will be presented to the Elder's Ministry for the approval as a qualified candidate for the office of elder.

### Election

Upon two-thirds vote of the Elder's Ministry, a quorum being present, each approved candidate shall be elected to the Elder's Ministry.

### Presentation to the body

The elders shall present the new member to the congregation at a regular meeting of the congregation.

## Process for the nomination of deacons

### Selection and approval of deacons

In the church where the leaders are deacons, the church membership will identify those who meet the biblical requirement outlined in 1 Timothy 3:8–12. After a candidate has been identified, the candidate and spouse will be invited to a personal interview. After a candidate has successfully completed the personal interview, the candidate will be invited to participate in the Deacon Training Program. Those who have been selected to participate in the training program will be presented before the church for affirmation. Those who successfully complete the Deacon's Training Program will be presented before the church in preparation for an ordination service.

### Ordination of deacons

Each deacon shall be ordained after successfully completing a year of supervised ministry training. After it is determined that the deacon in training has met all the spiritual and personal qualifications, an Ordination Service shall be conducted. At his service, the deacon shall receive the "laying on of hands" by the deacons to signify his acceptance and approval by the church.

## Conclusion

Let us all be committed to building up the kingdom of God in and through the church (Eph. 1:22–23). This will allow the power, authority and work of Christ, through the Holy Spirit, to be manifested to everyone. This process blesses our families and us. We must trust Him and allow Him to be head of the church (Col. 1:17–20) so that we can, through Him, impact lives in the church, the community and the world.

## DEVELOPING A TEAM OF VOLUNTEERS

### *Introduction*

In order for the vision of a pastor to become a functional part of the church, a volunteer force must be organized. This is not only essential for the expansion of the vision, it is also important for the spiritual health and strength in the church as well as the spiritual maturity of the believer (Eph. 4:12–13, 16). The Church of Sardis was accused by God for their lack of faithful service to him. God expected them to serve faithfully for the furtherance of the ministry (Rev. 2:1–3). A volunteer force is critical to a church's ministry.

Churches must begin to see that Christ sends members to their body (Acts 2:47) with spiritual gifts (1 Pet. 4:10) for the purpose of serving the needs of the saints. Each believer must be faithful (I Cor. 4:1–2) to this process because this determines how they will be rewarded in heaven (1 Cor. 3:10–15; 2 Cor. 5:10). When the church is focused in this manner, it becomes a workforce for the kingdom of God, blessing hurting people, rather than just a gathering of believers each week.

Because volunteers can effectively serve to expand the vision of the church, strengthen the spiritual life of the congregation by serving, and stimulate their own spiritual growth, the development of a volunteer force is one of the most essential aspects of church ministry.

### *The Motivation for Service*

There are several ways that members can become motivated for service as part of a team of volunteers in the church. They are as follows.

### *Through the teaching and preaching ministry of the church*

- Jesus developed the greatest volunteer ministry ever. He did this by teaching and training ordinary men to be His disciples, holding them accountable to their calling, impacting them personally, becoming their friend (someone whom they loved; John 21:1–14), and letting them be exposed to His ministry.

- The pastor should select sermon topics that challenge believers to service.

103

- The best kind of motivation, which serves as a blessing in a local church, should come from the inside of a believer. This process must be driven and directed by the development of the ministry of the Holy Spirit in the life of the believer (John 16:7–13). This occurs as a result of a discipleship ministry within the church.

## Through directing members to serve

### Membership Class

Along with teachings on the meaning of salvation, discipleship, and giving, the church should teach the Biblical meaning of the vision of the church. This should include a careful explanation of how the vision is worked out in the life of the church. The importance of this process is to create in each member their responsibility to share in the development of the agenda of Christ in the church, the community and the world.

All the ministries of the church should be put in a PowerPoint presentation so that members can become fully informed about the nature of the church's ministries as well as all the areas of need that each ministry may have. Each member is taught that they are expected to serve. This expectation is the Lord's expectation of them (1 Cor. 4:1–2; 3:10–15; 2 Cor. 5:10; Eph. 4:12–13).

### Spiritual Gifts Class

This class is designed to help members discover and use their spiritual gift(s), and emphasize their importance for spiritual development of the church. "As each one has received a special gift, employ it in serving one another as good steward of the manifold grace of God" (1 Pet. 4:10).

### Bible Study

Teach through books that emphasize the role of believers (Eph., Rev. 3:1–6, 14–22).

### Sunday School

Develop a Sunday School curriculum that is focused on maturing believers spiritually. A growing believer will sense their need to be commuted to the church. Choose curriculum that discusses spiritual gifts or the responsibility of believers to the local church.

### *Through orienting church ministries to the needs of people*

- Church leadership must demonstrate that they sincerely care for the needs of the members. This can be done in the following manner

    » Each deacon has several families that he cares for on a continual basis.

    » Each deacon will call their families at least once a month to pray for them and listen to their concerns.

    » Care for members, especially when they are hurting, through the Comfort and Care Ministry. This serves to motivate them to be committed to the church and its vision.

- Ministry leaders should lead their ministries as a deacon or church leader leads a care cell ministry. They can do so in the following manner:

    » When the leader begins their meetings, check to see if members have special prayer needs.

    » Follow up when committee members are missing.

    » Visit members when they are hospitalized. Send them cards for birthdays, anniversaries, the birth of a child, etc. Christ became a part of the life of Peter by healing his mother-in-law (Luke 4:38), and blessing his business with his best fishing day (Luke 5:6–8). As a result of this, as well as Christ's teaching ministry, Peter dropped everything and followed Christ.

        This simple fact requires that you figure out a way to keep the interest and motivation of each person high and at the same time help those who are more on fire to develop to the maximum.[2]

2. Leroy Eims, *Be the Leader You Were Meant to Be: Growing Into the Leader God Called You to Be* (Wheaton: Victor, 1975), 134–135.

***Allow members to serve in areas of ministry that are natural for them***

- Allow members, if they do not know their spiritual gifts, to serve in an area they believe they like for six months to one year. Let them know that they can change ministry areas after that period.

- If a member works with computers or does accounting, the church leadership should allow them to start there. As they build relationships in the church and become more a part of the body, they will want to branch out to different ministries in the church.

- In Luke 5:1–11, Christ reached out to Peter, then told him that He wanted him to fish for men.

***Mobilization of Members for Service***

- The vision of the church should be clear to everyone who joins the church. It should be placed in the bulletin or in a visible place in the church. The motto should be somewhere visible in the sanctuary.

- A ministry plan that is organized allows each member to play a significant role in the development of the vision.

- Twice a year, have a "Ministry Fair" that showcases all the ministries of the church and relates them to the major objectives of the vision. This highlights the major ministries and what they do. Have tables around the church to encourage members to sign up for ministry areas after service. Cancel Sunday School that morning to maximize attendance. During the "Ministry Fair," allow members to switch ministries if they have been in one for six months to a year.

- Have ministry highlights at least two Sundays per month. This allows each major ministry to be highlighted so that people are attracted to serve. Follow up with each person who signed up by phone and card, challenging them to come to an orientation meeting.

- Establish a newsletter that does the following:

  » Highlights the needs of each ministry.

  » Exposes members to the various activities of each ministry.

  » Exposes members to some of the positive results of various ministries.

## CONCLUSION

In order for any church to accomplish its goals, there must be a strong team. This is crucial to the strength and continued growth of the church. When people feel they are a significant part of the church, they will probably remain at the church for a long time. Persons who are just attending church and are not involved eventually leave. So along with assisting the church in fulfilling its vision, a volunteer force also allows the church to maintain its membership.

A strong leadership team, combined with an effective volunteer force, allows a church to individually and collectively grow to the fullness of Christ for the glory of God (Eph. 4:12–16). Without members serving, the church becomes stagnant and ineffective. The few who are serving burn out or they become more focused on accomplishing a task than caring for people.

## Chapter Eight

# STAFFING THE STRATEGY

Staffing the strategy is just as important as developing a strategy. A person can have a great strategy but the wrong foot soldiers, rendering the strategy of little effect. The selection of leadership must remain biblically based and these individuals must be dedicated to the Lord and the leadership He has established in the church. It is better for a pastor to take his time (which includes a lot of prayer) to put leaders in place, than to be so committed to the implementation of the vision that he undermines his own vision because he rushes and puts the wrong leaders in various positions.

The Bible states it this way; "Do not lay hands upon anyone too hastily and thereby share responsibility for the sins of others keep yourself free from sin" (1 Tim. 5:22). Following the vision provided in this book, and the strategy developed from it, here are some Ministry Descriptions (Job Descriptions) for the major ministry areas. They may serve as guidelines to assist in staffing the vision:

## FAMILY MINISTRY—MINISTRY DESCRIPTION

### *Principal Function*

The principal function of this ministry is to seek to minister to the diverse needs of families. The focus is to grow family members closer to God and to each other. This ministry seeks to outline the biblical roles of the family and challenges all members of each family to support God's rule for the home. It provides counseling as well as financial planning for all families who seek assistance from this ministry area. This ministry serves as the counseling center for all issues presented to church leadership.

## *Qualifications*

- Must have evidence of a personal relationship with Jesus Christ and demonstrate consistent progress toward spiritual maturity.

- Must have a master's degree from a Bible College or seminary. Has taken significant amount of classes in counseling and family development.

- Must be an ordained minister who can validate his call to the ministry.

- Must be a member of the church.

- Must have an observable commitment to the goals of this ministry and the overall vision of the church.

- Must have a teachable spirit.

- Must be committed to be a spiritual example to other believers in the church.

- Must have good administrative skills.

- Must have a transferable knowledge of central Bible doctrines and the truths necessary to provide effective leadership to the department.

- Must have evidence of a commitment to Biblical principles in regard to counseling techniques.

## *Ministry Responsibilities*

Work in a team relationship with other church leaders so that in the presence or absence of the pastor, the leadership of the church functions in a cohesive manner. Must always keep the vision in mind, the objectives for that particular activity and what directions the pastor may have provided.

- Committed to attend Bible Study and worship regularly and be involved in most of the church's activities.

- Oversee the implementation of all activities that are on the church calendar. This involves updating, during staff meeting, and associate pastors' meetings, the status of activities for each month. This is done for each month, prior to the beginning of the month.

- Organize and provide counseling for couples or single parents that request counseling.

- Organize and/or provide pre-marital counseling.

- Create an environment around the church that would lead couples to work on their relationships and become deeply committed to developing strong family structures.

- Work with the Life Application Ministry to organize classes on marriage.

- Encourage couples to attend activities that are part of the Family Ministry. These activities are outlined in the Family Ministry organizational charts.

- Organize the family ministry to deal with the diverse needs of the families of the church. This includes dealing with single parenting issues.

- Notify pastor upon receiving information that a couple is considering divorce.

- Organize the support groups and/or counseling for widows/widowers as well as divorced individuals.

- Organize workshops or seminars that would serve to assist families with their financial needs.

- Recruiting members to accomplish Family Ministry objectives.

- Attend Life Application Classes consistently, unless attendance conflicts with another ministry activity.

- Attend worship and Bible study consistently.

- Show commitment to preserve the unity of the body.

- Complete other assigned duties as outlined by the pastor.

### *Organizational Relationship*

Is directly accountable to the senior pastor and is responsible for the execution of his prescribed duties.

### *Associate Pastor of Shepherding Ministry—Ministry Description*
**Principal Function**

This position is focused on making sure every member is accounted for, cared for and the leaders are developed to serve the diverse needs of God's people. It is to also ensure that the pastor is properly represented when members are hurting and in need of experiencing God's love. It is to ensure that all elders' and deacons' retreats, as well as training programs for ministers are properly organized for the glory of God.

**Qualifications**

- Evidence of a personal relationship with Jesus Christ and demonstrate consistent progress toward spiritual maturity.

- Master's degree from a Bible College or seminary.

- Ordained minister who can validate his call to the ministry.

- Member of the church.

- Observable commitment to the goals of this ministry and the overall vision of the church.

- Committed to be spiritual example to other believers in the church.

- Strong administrative skills.

- Transferable knowledge of central Bible doctrines and truths necessary to provide effective leadership to the department.

- Evidence of a commitment to biblical principles in regard to counseling techniques.

**Ministry Responsibilities**

- Meet with ministry coordinators for prayer, discipleship discussions and ministry development issues.

- Ensure that coordinators are attending coordinator meetings regularly.

- Attend Life Application Classes consistently, unless attendance conflicts with another ministry activity.

- Attend worship and Bible study consistently.

- Show commitment to preserve the unity of the body.

**Shepherding New Members**

- This position works with the Deacon Coordinator and the New Membership Coordinator to assign families to the deacons. The ministry team leaders must maintain contact until their new deacons have contacted each new member.

- If a new member becomes sick during the time they are in new membership classes, the associate pastor of the Shepherding Ministry must work with the New Membership Deacon, the Comfort and Care Ministry, and maybe Ministry Team leaders to serve the needs of this member.

- If a new member no longer shows up for new membership classes or church, the Search and Rescue Coordinator or the deacon for that particular member must seek to contact and assess the new member's status.

- When church discipline becomes necessary, this ministry is responsible for working with the Discipleship Ministry to do the following:

  » Keeping the individual that has been disciplined before the prayer committee. They must pray that the member repents and humbles him- or herself for the restoration process.

  » Contacting the individual from time to time to see how they are doing. This is an effort to demonstrate that the church still cares and would love to see them walk right before God again.

  » Establish a restoration process, in cooperation with the Discipleship Ministry so that each member is fully restored back into the life of the church. This may consist of the following:

    › Assign a same-gender discipler, who has been trained through the Guidance Ministry, to the disciplined believer.

    › The discipler will serve as an accountability partner.

**This ministry organizes baptism in the following manner**

- Make sure all baptism candidates, whether adult or children, go through the baptism class.

  » The children's pastor teaches children.

114

> » Young adults by the young adult pastor.

> » Youth by youth pastor.

> » Adults are cared for through the Associate Pastor for Shepherding Ministry.

- Make sure each member gets a certificate.

- Make sure each new member understands what clothing they should wear.

- Work with Administration to make sure the pool is set up and rooms are made available for people who need to change.

**Shepherding Members**

- Visit members who are in the hospital as a representation of the pastor and the church.

- Keep up with members who are homebound with regular visits and calls; provision of sermon tapes and devotional material; and by making sure that the deacons are going by to share the Lord's Supper.

- Develop and train individuals in the Comfort and Care ministry to make sure it is functioning according to the ministry outline.

- Oversee the Deacon Fellowship to make sure every aspect of this ministry is organized to achieve the ministry goals. Make sure that the deacons (working along with the Deacon Coordinator) are recruiting coordinators to properly manage the Deacon Fellowships.

- Make sure that all deacons' meetings are properly planned and organized so that the Bible study time is properly done, the coordinators are there on time, and the meetings function to achieve ministry goals.

- Make sure the Administrative Deacons are properly trained and are functioning based on ministry guidelines.

- Work with Comfort and Care and Deacons' Ministries during the time of bereavement so that families are properly supported.

  » Send a card a week or two after someone has lost a loved one (include the pastor's name). About a month later, call the person to check on them.

  » If the person is widowed, keep up with them through cards and phone calls.

  » If the person is a senior that is widowed, work with the Associate Pastor of Fellowship to get the Silver Star ministry to be supportive to this member.

- Work with the prayer ministry so that it achieves its ministry goals. This includes but is not limited to prayer vigils, and prayer request distribution to elders and deacons. Work with deacons and their coordinators to encourage families to participate. Seek to organize deacons to each take one hour of the prayer vigils.

**Leadership and Ministry Related Issues**
- Make sure that deacons are properly trained for ministry. This includes but is not limited to the following:

  » Preparation of deacon materials.

  » Scheduling of meeting times/rooms.

  » Assignment to a mentor.

  » Ensure deacons' faithful service.

- This is done in collaboration with the elder responsible for training deacons.

- Work with the Leadership and Conference Coordinator to make sure all leadership workshops, retreats and conferences are properly planned, organized and executed.

- Recruit members so that this area is able to achieve its objectives.

**Accountability**
- Directly accountable to the senior pastor and the assistant pastor.

- Directly responsible for all areas outlined in the ministry charts.

**Desired Outcome of the Job**
- Ministry area is operating smoothly, ethically and efficiently.

- The pastor is represented before members who are hurting and are in need of emotional and spiritual support.

- Needs of God's people are met.

- Leaders are properly prepared for ministry.

**Pastoral Responsibilities**
- Assist the pastor and the assistant pastor with counseling as needed.

- Assist the pastor with worship responsibilities on Sunday.

- Assist the pastor with members who call the church needing counseling during times the pastor is unavailable.

- Assist the pastor, when necessary, with hospital visitation, bereavement or Comfort and Care ministry.

**Organizational Relationship**
The associate pastor of shepherding is accountable to the senior pastor and the assistant pastor and is directly responsible for all staff that is assigned to assist in the execution of these prescribed duties.

### *Associate Pastor of the Fellowship Ministry – Ministry Description*
**Principal Function**

Principal function is to organize fellowship activities that are designed to promote interpersonal caring and sharing of God's people with one another as an outgrowth of our fellowship with God, as well as to stimulate believers to grow spiritually so that the church demonstrates the personality of Christ. This is not only accomplished through fellowship activities but also the singles', men's, women's and young adult ministries.

**Qualifications**

- Evidence of a personal relationship with Jesus Christ and demonstrate a consistent aptitude for spiritual maturity.

- Bachelor's or a master's degree from a Bible College or seminary.

- Member of the church.

- Observable commitment to the goals of this ministry and the overall vision of the church.

- Committed to be a spiritual example to other believers in the church.

- Strong administrative skills.

- Transferable knowledge of central Bible doctrines and the truths necessary to provide effective leadership to the ministry.

- Evidence of a commitment to biblical principles in regard to counseling techniques.

- Ability to speak to groups and prepare necessary materials for trainings.

- Ability to work closely with staff responsible for the various ministries.

- Committed to the doctrinal positions of the church.

- Proven flexibility, creativity, and spontaneity in program design.

**Ministry Responsibilities**

- Directing and coordinating all ministry areas as outlined in this ministry chart.

- Training and supervising the activities of all the coordinators and teachers for this ministry.

- Develop atmosphere of mutual love, appreciation and respect with activities such as Family Funships, Silver Star Ministry, Sports Ministry, the Young Adults, Singles,' Men's and Women's ministries.

- Assist in recruitment, and training of all leadership staff functioning in this area of the church's ministry.

- Work with other ministries to organize cost-effective food purchase and preparation for various activities, for example taking advantage of bulk food purchases. Deacon Family Fellowship activities are included in this function.

- Promote family and group participation by challenging members to participate in various athletic programs. Work with the Singles', Men's and Women's Ministries to provide assistance in the planning and executing of their ministry goals and objectives.

- Work with the annual event coordinator to make sure that the church's picnic is properly planned, promoted and executed.

- Work to develop an effective cross-cultural ministry with churches in the community so that the church body exemplifies love in a manner that glorifies God.

- Oversee the sports activities that are sponsored by the church to promote fellowship and unity among members of the church, as well as develop church teams that may compete with outside agency or churches.

- Attend Life Application Classes consistently, unless attendance conflicts with another ministry activity.

- Attend worship and Bible study consistently.

- Show commitment to preserve the unity of the body.

- Perform other duties as assigned.

**Pastoral Responsibilities**

- Assist the pastor and the assistant pastor with counseling as needed.

- Assist the pastor with worship responsibilities on Sunday.

- Assist the pastor with members who call the church needing counseling during times the pastor is unavailable.

- Assist the pastor, when necessary, with hospital visitation, bereavement or out Comfort and Care ministry.

### Organizational Relationship

The associate pastor of fellowship is accountable to the senior pastor and the assistant pastor and is directly responsible for all staff that is assigned to assist in the execution of his prescribed duties.

## Associate Pastor of the Worship Ministry—Ministry Description
### Principal Ministry

The associate pastor of worship is responsible for the effective organization and direction of the Worship Ministries of the church and worship responsibilities at Tuesday Bible Study. He will seek to develop an exciting worship atmosphere that serves to encourage worshippers to focus on glorifying God in spirit and in truth.

## Qualifications

- Must have evidence of a personal relationship with Jesus Christ and demonstrate consistent progress toward spiritual maturity. Must seek to be a part of a Spiritual Growth Class and Bible Study.

- Must be an ordained minister who can validate his call to the ministry.

- Must be a member of the church.

- Must have an observable commitment to the goals of this ministry and the overall vision of the church.

- Must have some formal training for music, whether it is an associate's degree or bachelor's degree.

- Must have training in music and in voice.

- Must have experience directing church choirs.

- Must be skilled in leading children as well as adults.

- Must be able to play piano and organ.

- Must know how to play various types of music.

- Must be able to work the established hours.

- Must be committed to be a spiritual example to other believers in the church.

- Must have good administrative skills.

- Must have transferable knowledge of central Bible doctrines and truths necessary to provide effective leadership to the department.

- Must have evidence of a commitment to biblical principles in regard to counseling techniques.

**Ministry Responsibilities**
- Must work with worship leaders to coordinate worship as outlined in the worship ministry chart. Make sure worship leaders work with a spirit of unity and with a commitment to worship God sincerely.

- Responsible for developing a comprehensive and balanced music program for the church.

- Responsible for conducting praise and worship each Sunday, and training and preparing the praise and worship team for each Sunday.

- Responsible for giving the praise scripture, order of worship and overheads ready for worship whether present or absent. This must include songs during the Lord's Supper.

- Responsible for making sure that worship starts promptly each Sunday. Must work with other ministry leaders to make sure worship starts on time.

- Is responsible for recruiting members so that this area is able to achieve its objectives.

- Responsible to ensure that all choirs (adult, young adult, children and youth) have proper direction and leadership, and are prepared to sing each Sunday.

- Responsible for leading the congregation in praise and worship on Tuesday nights.

- Must show leadership by being on time to conduct all music as well as being on time for worship service.

- Responsible for working with administration to ensure all church music instruments and audio equipment is maintained.

- Responsible for hiring and training musicians so that the music ministry functions with the vision of the church.

- In the pastor's absence must work with the assistant pastor in an effort to fulfill ministry responsibilities.

- Must work with the budget committee to assist in developing a functional budget for the Music Ministry.

- Must work with the Audio Ministry to ensure that the mike system is properly coordinated with the Music Ministry for an effective worship experience. The same preparation should also be given to the Video Ministry.

- Assist with answering the phone when in the office.

- Responsible to attend staff meetings if regular work schedule does not conflict.

- Responsible for coordinating Worship Team meeting once every month. Work diligently to develop a unified team of individuals, who will work in harmony for genuine worship before God.

- Attend Life Application Classes consistently, unless attendance conflicts with another ministry activity.

- Attend worship and Bible study consistently.

- Show commitment to preserve the unity of the body.

- Perform other duties as assigned.

**Pastoral Responsibilities**
- Assist the pastor and the assistant pastor with any counseling as needed.

- Assist the pastor with worship responsibilities on Sunday.

- Assist the pastor with members who call the church needing counseling.

- Assist the pastor, when necessary, with hospital visitation, bereavement or Comfort and Care ministry.

**Organizational Relationship**

The associate pastor of worship is accountable to the senior pastor and the assistant pastor and is directly responsible for all staff that is assigned to assist in the execution of his prescribed duties.

## *Associate Pastor of the Discipleship Ministry—Job Description*
**Principal Function**

The principal function of this position is to oversee the continual development of all the ministries associated with the Discipleship Ministry. This includes, but is not limited to the New Membership, Life Application, Counseling, Spiritual Gifts, Reconciliation and Women ministries. This includes training and disciplining coordinators that will assist the discipleship pastor in the discipleship ministry.

**Qualifications**

- Evidence of a personal relationship with Jesus Christ and demonstrate a consistent aptitude for spiritual maturity.

- Master's degree from a Bible College or seminary.

- Ordained minister who can validate his call to the ministry

- Prepared to be a member of the church.

- Observable commitment to the goals of this ministry and the overall vision of the church.

- Committed to be a spiritual example to other believers in the church.

- Strong administrative skills.

- Transferable knowledge of central Bible doctrines and truths necessary to provide effective leadership to the ministry.

- Evidence of a commitment to biblical principles in regard to counseling techniques.

- Committed to the doctrinal positions of the church.

**Ministry Responsibilities**

- Research and secure materials to effectively meet the spiritual needs of members in the Discipleship Ministry, and to ensure that members are equipped to handle the ongoing challenges in life and ministry.

- Work with the pastor to structure and develop new membership classes.

- Train ministry coordinators and teachers, and meet with them for prayer each Sunday before Life Application Classes begin.

- Work regularly with teachers for continuing education classes.

- Must work with the counseling ministry to ensure that members are restored or equipped in challenging periods of their lives.

- Developing activities that will serve to develop genuine relationships among the members involved in Life Application Classes.

- Recruit members to achieve ministry objectives.

- Coordinate the Reconciliation Ministry that is designed to restore members who have been caught in a trespass (Galatians 6:1) or assist members who need spiritual guidance as they resolve conflicts.

- Coordinate the Spiritual Gifts Ministry to help members discover their gift(s). These members must then be assimilated into a ministry so that each member serves the purpose outlined in Ephesians 4:12–16.

- Assist the pastor and assistant pastor in the provision of Pastoral Care to the church members as well as provide counseling as needed.

- Work with the pastor and assistant pastor in coordinating the support ministries of the church.

- In cooperation with the Deacon Fellowships, and the Shepherding Associate Pastor, develop home Bible Studies so that members who "play" together can grow together. The pastor must approve each teacher.

- Meet with committee heads once every month.

- Annually or upon request, provide Discipleship Ministry budget updates.

- Attend Life Application Classes consistently, unless attendance conflicts with another ministry activity.

- Attend worship and Bible study consistently.

- Show commitment to preserve the unity of the body.

- Perform other duties as assigned.

**Pastoral Responsibilities**

- Assist the pastor and the assistant pastor with counseling as needed.

- Assist the pastor with worship responsibilities on Sunday.

- Assist the pastor with counseling duties, hospital visitation, bereavement and Comfort and Care ministry.

### Organizational Relationship

This discipleship associate pastor is accountable to the senior pastor as well as the assistant pastor and is directly responsible for all staff that is assigned to assist in the execution of his prescribed duties.

## *Associate Pastor of the Children and Youth Ministry—Ministry Description*

### Principal Function

The principal function of this position is to oversee the continual development of all the ministries in this area so that they accomplish its goals and objectives consistent with the ministry philosophy. This includes, but is not limited to AWANA, Children's Neighborhood Programs, children's ministries, and supervising the development of the day-to-day operations of the youth ministry. This includes training and discipling coordinators to provide assistance.

### Qualifications

- Personal relationship with Jesus Christ and demonstrate a consistent aptitude for spiritual maturity.

- Bachelors or master's degree from a Bible College or seminary.

- Ordained minister who can validate his call to the ministry.

- Prepared to become a member of the church.

- Observable commitment to the goals of this ministry and the overall vision of the church.

- Committed to be a spiritual example to other believers in the church.

- Strong administrative skills.

- Transferable knowledge of central Bible doctrines and truths necessary to provide effective leadership to the ministry.

- Evidence of a commitment to Biblical principles in regard to counseling techniques.

- Committed to the doctrinal positions of the church.

**Ministry Responsibilities**

- Direction and coordination of all ministry areas as outlined in the ministry chart.

- Training and supervising ministry coordinators and teachers .

- Research, develop, secure and coordinate curricular and extra-curricular materials that will deepen members' knowledge of the Word of God so that they can effectively serve. This includes children's and youth ministry curriculum/development.

- Training of qualified coordinators, teachers, activity workers and support workers.

- Develop neighborhood programs such as Bible Clubs, Summer Vacation Bible School (V.B.S.), and AWANA for the community and Apartment Bible Clubs in an effort to win children to Christ and grow them spiritually.

- Recruit members to achieve ministry objectives.

- Meet with committee heads at least once every month, focus on developing coordinators spiritually.

- Provide budgetary needs for the ministry for the annual budget or upon request.

- Attend Life Application Classes consistently, unless attendance conflicts with another ministry activity.

- Attend worship and Bible study consistently.

- Show commitment to preserve the unity of the body.

- Perform other duties as assigned.

**Pastoral Responsibilities**

- Assist the pastor and the assistant pastor with counseling as needed.

- Assist the pastor with worship responsibilities on Sunday.

- Assist the pastor with members who call the church needing counseling during times the pastor is unavailable.

- Assist the pastor, when necessary, with hospital visitation, bereavement or the Comfort and Care ministry.

**Organizational Relationship**
The children and youth ministry associate pastor is accountable to the senior pastor and the assistant pastor and is directly responsible for all staff that is assigned to assist in the execution of his prescribed duties in the church.

## *Youth Minister—Ministry description*
**Principal Function**
To oversee the continued development of the youth ministry and the discipleship of youth to engage in effective worship and deeply commit to integrating God's Word into their lives through counseling, leadership development, evangelism and fellowship.

**Qualifications**

- Member of the church.

- Demonstrate a deep commitment to grow spiritually.

- Passion to nurture young people to spiritual maturity and challenge them to repeat the process with others.

- Committed to follow the vision and direction of the senior pastor.

- Committed to the doctrinal beliefs of the church.

- Bachelor's degree with a training emphasis in Youth Ministries.

- Demonstrated commitment to church leadership, as well as a commitment to preserve the unity of the body.

- Attend worship and Bible Study consistently.

- Strong organizational skills.

**Responsibilities**
- Maintain office hours, complete reports on a timely basis, attend weekly staff meetings and monthly associate pastors' meetings.

- Primary direction, oversight, and teaching under the leadership of the pastor, assistant pastor and associate pastor of the Children and Youth Ministry.

- Counsel youth when necessary.

- Develop effective relationships with parents.

- Teach Bible and Chapel at Inwood Oaks Christian School.

- Organize evangelism/outreach activities to teach young people how to share their faith and minister to the diverse needs of the community.

- Develop and grow a dynamic worship service that challenges youth to worship the Lord sincerely and begin to transition into adult worship.

- Work with the associate pastor of worship to develop a dynamic youth month (August of each year) which includes, but is not limited to, their involvement in the adult worship service.

- Adhere to the guidelines, policies, doctrinal statement, and the code of conduct of the church based on the Word of God.

- Recruit members to achieve ministry objectives

- Begin and end each youth activity with prayer.

- Plan, organize, coordinate and direct the Youth Ministry activities and administration.

- Work with the young adult director to coordinate a smooth transition from children to youth to young adult ministry.

- Recruit and develop parents and members to assist in the organization and implementation of youth ministry activities.

- Assist other staff ministers, office staff, and other ministries on request.

- Attend Life Application Classes consistently, unless attendance conflicts with another ministry activity.

- Attend worship and Bible study consistently.

- Show commitment to preserve the unity of the body.

- Perform other duties as assigned.

**Organizational Commitment**

The youth minister is accountable to the children and youth associate pastor, senior pastor and the assistant pastor and is directly responsible for all staff that is assigned to assist in the execution of his prescribed duties.

## *Young Adult Pastor—Ministry Description*

**Principal Function**

To direct and oversee the spiritual, academic, vocational, emotional, and social growth and development of the young adults, ages 18–25, of the church by the relevant application of God's Word to real life issues through the means of life-example, teaching, preaching, counseling, vision-casting, leading, outreach, and discipleship (1 Tim. 4:6–16).

### Qualifications

- Evidence of a personal relationship with Jesus Christ and a consistent aptitude for spiritual maturity.

- Bachelor's degree from a Bible College.

- Ordained minister who can validate his call to the ministry.

- Prepared to be member of the church.

- Observable commitment to the goals of this ministry and the overall vision of the church.

- Committed to be a spiritual example to other believers in the church.

- Strong administrative skills.

- Transferable knowledge of central Bible doctrines and truths necessary to provide effective leadership to the ministry.

- Evidence of a commitment to biblical principles in regard to counseling techniques.

- Committed to the doctrinal positions of the church.

### Ministry Responsibilities

- Organize and implement the development of the vision of the Young Adult Ministry.

- Primary direction, oversight, and teaching of the Young Adult ministry.

- Coordinate and direct the activities, administration, Bible studies, leadership training and development, and the Sunday Worship service of the young adult ministry.

- Meet counseling and discipleship needs of the young adults in the church.

- Keep an active list of young adults who are in college and engage in regular communications and activities when they are home for the purpose of relationship development and sharing of common struggles with a focus on God's Word.

- Teach a Life Application class that would serve the needs of the young adults and develop leaders.

- Develop regular monthly activities that would serve to build healthy relationships.

- Provide the church staff with office hours (20 per week) and reports of progress and needs at the weekly staff meetings on Tuesday afternoons.

- Assist other staff ministers and ministries when necessary and when requested.

- Adhere to the guidelines, policies, doctrinal statement, and code of conduct of the church, based on the Word of God.

- Develop annual Youth Ministry budget, and provide budget updates and needs on request.

- Attend Life Application Classes consistently, unless attendance conflicts with another ministry activity.

- Attend worship and Bible study consistently.

- Show commitment to preserve the unity of the body.

- Perform other duties as assigned.

**Pastoral Responsibilities**

- Assist the pastor and the assistant pastor with any counseling as needed.

- Assist the pastor with worship responsibilities on Sunday.

- Assist the pastor with counseling needs of the congregation.

- Assist the pastor, when necessary, with hospital visitation, bereavement or the Comfort and Care ministry.

**Organizational Relationship**

The young adult pastor is accountable to the senior pastor as well as the assistant pastor and is directly responsible for all staff that is assigned to assist in the execution of his prescribed duties.

## Associate Pastor of Evangelism and Missions—Ministry Description

**Principal Function**

The principal function of this position is to oversee the continual development of all related ministries so that goals and objectives are accomplished consistently with the ministry philosophy. It is to also to challenge the church body to be involved in evangelism and missions, and to consistently keep the church body informed and involved of what is going on as a result of the activities of the Neighborhood Evangelistic Team. This position is responsible for overseeing the development and execution of all mission trips and to keep the overall church body involved in preparing, praying and assisting all mission teams with each trip.

**Qualifications**

- Evidence of a personal relationship with Jesus Chris and demonstrate a consistent aptitude for spiritual maturity.

- Bachelors or master's degree from a Bible College or seminary.

- Ordained minister who can validate his call to the ministry.

- Prepared to become a member of the church.

- Observable commitment to the goals of this ministry and the overall vision of the church.

- Committed to be a spiritual example to other believers in the church.

- Strong administrative skills.

- Transferable knowledge of central Bible doctrines and truths necessary to provide effective leadership to the ministry.

- Evidence of a commitment to biblical principles in regard to counseling techniques.

- Committed to the doctrinal position of the church.

**Ministry Responsibilities**

- Direct and coordinate all ministry areas as outlined in the ministry chart for Evangelism and Missions Ministry.

- Training and supervising the activities of coordinators and teachers for this ministry.

- Research and secure materials (evangelistic tracts, etc.) that will effectively deepen members' knowledge of the Word of God so that they can effectively serve in this ministry area.

- Make sure all mission trips are well organized, and the team is well prepared before being sent out. While the team is out on a mission trip keep the church body updated on how the team is doing.

- Work with the mission coordinator to organize and plan Missions Month each year. Work with pastor to find a speaker.

- Work with evangelism coordinator to make sure the second Sunday team outreach efforts are well-coordinated and they have the proper material and training.

- Keep the congregation challenged to become involved in evangelism and missions.

- Work with the missions coordinator to make sure all missionaries are properly supported and to evaluate new requests.

- Provide well-trained team of individuals to the Jail and Prison Ministry, and handle outreach logistics and program content.

- Work with Children and Youth ministry when they have evangelistic efforts. Assist them in finding adult volunteers for their efforts.

- Coordinate all the transportation needs of this ministry area. Work with administration to make sure vans are properly prepared and equipped for each trip.

- Plan and implement evangelism workshops for the entire church at least once every year.

- Work with the Special Outreach Project Coordinator to ensure church involvement in these one-time activities.

- Work with the Christian Outreach Center to provide evangelistic materials for outreach activities or events.

- Work with the counseling ministry to provide follow-up and assistance on Sunday when individuals come forward to accept Christ.

- Attend Life Application Classes consistently, unless attendance conflicts with another ministry activity.

- Attend worship and Bible study consistently.

- Show commitment to preserve the unity of the body.

- Perform other duties as assigned.

**Pastoral Responsibilities**

- Assist the pastor and assistant pastor with any counseling as needed.

- Assist the pastor with worship responsibilities on Sunday.

- Assist the pastor with counseling needs.

- Assist the pastor, when necessary, with hospital visitation, bereavement or the Comfort and Care ministry.

**Organizational Relationship**

The associate pastor of evangelism and missions is accountable to the pastor and assistant pastor.

## *Christian Outreach Center Director—Ministry Description*
**Principal Function**

The principal function for this area is to develop outreach ministries to powerfully impact the community. This ministry involves training co-ordinators and mentors to effectively meet community needs and change lives. Develop future programs through the ministry of the Director of Development. Organize the use of the Christian Outreach Center so that it serves the community in an effective manner.

The outreach director, along with the pastor, coordinates the development and function of the Christian Outreach Center Board of Directors.

**Qualifications**

- Evidence of a personal relationship with Jesus Christ and demonstrate a consistent aptitude for spiritual maturity.

- Bachelors or master's degree from a Bible college or seminary.

- Experience in development and directing outreach ministries.

- Member of the church.

- Observable commitment to the goals of this ministry and the overall vision of the church.

- Committed to be a spiritual example to other believers in the church.

- Strong administrative skills.

- Transferable knowledge of central Bible doctrine and truths necessary to provide effective leadership to the ministry.

- Evidence of a commitment to biblical principles in regard to counseling techniques.

- Ability to speak to groups and prepare necessary materials for trainings.

- Experience handling family crises with sensitivity.

- Ability to be a leader to staff and clients.

- Committed to the doctrinal positions of the church.

- Knowledge of all aspects of operations of the Outreach Center so there is a good understanding of the center.

- Respect for and understanding of client confidentiality from a legal and a spiritual perspective.

- Strong communication and organizational skills.

- Proven flexibility, creativity, and spontaneity in program design.

- Public speaking experience.

**Ministry Responsibilities**

- Directing and coordinating all ministry areas as outlined in the ministry chart.

- Training and supervising the activities of all the coordinators and teachers for this ministry, including research into innovative training materials.

- Communicate with the Administrative Ministry to make sure the building is properly maintained.

- Counselors and mentors that can effectively serve the needs of the community from a biblical perspective.

- Represent The Christian Outreach Center at meetings and seminars as requested, to include public speaking presentations.

- Recruiting members to achieve ministry objectives.

- Attend weekly staff meetings as requested.

- Work with the pastor to make sure the food and clothing pantries are adequately stocked.

- Work with the Probation Department and P.A.C.E to maintain good relationships so that these collaborative efforts effectively impact the community.

- Work with volunteers to effectively minister to the needs of substance abusers from a Christian perspective.

- Interact with pastors and community leaders in an effort to develop collaborative efforts that would impact the community.

- Develop and coordinate Outreach Ministry activity calendar.

- Develop and maintain good relations with the community, including schools, hospitals, churches, social service agencies and inter-agency coalitions.

- Work with the director of development to establish the future programs of the church as well as secure grants from foundations in the areas of Housing Redevelopment, Economic Development, and Human and Social Services.

- Develop a Political Action Committee that serves to help the church body vote intelligently and to invite politicians to a forum so that members of the church and the community can be fully informed.

- Meet with committee heads at least once every month focusing on developing coordinators spiritually for the glory of God.

- Knowledge of community service agencies, domestic abuse laws, health service law, and other legislation/policies regarding homeless and sexually-assaulted clients.

- Maintain rapport with police departments, court system, Texas Workforce, Gulf Coast Careers, community agencies and community churches.

- Develop and present proposed Christian Outreach Center annual budget and updates upon request; review monthly for compliance.

- Oversee the development and regular updates of the Outreach Center Procedures Manual.

- Continually assess program needs; identify gaps and implement corrections; develop programs and/or areas for growth.

- Oversee maintenance of records and preparation of necessary reports relevant to Outreach programs.

- Attend Life Application Classes consistently, unless attendance conflicts with another ministry activity.

- Attend worship and Bible study consistently.

- Show commitment to preserve the unity of the body.

- Perform other duties as assigned.

**Organizational Relationship**
The Christian Outreach Center director is accountable to the senior pastor and the assistant pastor and is directly responsible for Center staff.

## Church Business Manager – Ministry Description
**Principal Function**
The church business manager will provide overall managerial leadership and give direction for support to the staff to accomplish the ministry goals of the church and auxiliary ministries. He/she will oversee the properties of the church following policies and guidelines established by the senior pastor and/or the elders.

**Qualifications**

- Born-again Christians with an evidenced walk with Christ. Give evidence of the fruit of the Spirit as a result of living and walking by the Spirit.

- Bachelor's degree in Business with classes in Accounting.

- Minimum one year of experience in business administration and management.

- Strong verbal, written communication and leadership skills.

- Strong personal discipline and organizational skills.

- Flexibility and creativity to respond positively to changes that may occur in a growing environment.

- Ability to work without direct supervision.

- Cooperate in all team efforts of planning, oversight and leadership.

- Ability to keep confidential data.

- Professional demeanor.

**Responsibilities**

- Maintain the church policies and all the church's facilities.

- Provide for the use of church facilities through an efficient scheduling and setup system.

- Is responsible for maintaining church properties, permits and procedural instructional manuals.

- Work with the associate pastors, outreach director and school superintendent to schedule activities at the church and school building.

- Maintain computer systems in all buildings.

- Ensure compliance with security processes and procedures for the church, school and outreach activities.

- Recruit members to assist in achieving objectives.

- Review and maintain the church's employee manual and records.

- Maintain proper office decorum and provide an atmosphere of efficiency and professionalism.

- Initiate and fulfill team goals and ensure cooperation among leadership, staff and members.

- Work with the accountant to maintain efficient, and effective management of routine expenditures. Maintain spending controls as directed by the pastor.

- Assist pastor and treasurer with developing presenting monthly budget reports to the elders and annual budget to membership, including church and school budgets.

- Negotiate for low prices with vendors.

- Maintain positive bank relationship.

- Supervise development of building committee(s) established by the pastor, and oversee ongoing building projects as needed for consistency with church policy.

- Assist in making deposits for the school.

- Supervise all aspects of building and grounds maintenance functions.

- Coordinate the scheduling of cleaning, maintenance, inspections insurance, van records and use of all church vehicles. Make sure that all community service workers are functioning properly.

- Work with the Parking Lot Committee to make sure volunteers are recruited, trained and are on the job at the appropriate times.

- Every Sunday, in cooperation with the church treasurer, ensure that the count team is in place and functioning based on the church's policy.

- Make sure all bulk mailings are properly organized and distributed.

- Oversee the development and distribution of the church newsletters.

- Attend Life Application Classes consistently, unless attendance conflicts with another ministry activity.

- Attend worship and Bible study consistently.

- Show commitment to preserve the unity of the body.

- Other tasks as assigned.

**Accountability**

- Is directly responsible to the senior pastor and the assistant pastor.

- Is directly responsible for the accountant, Sunday Count Team, office manager, receptionist, and maintenance staff.

- Must work with the outreach pastor and school superintendent to manage appropriate responsibilities at the Outreach Center and school buildings.

- Must maintain all church properties including vans and buses.

- Directly responsible for the proper operation of church finances.

**Desired Job Outcomes**

- A church that is operating smoothly, ethically and efficiently.

- Facilities that are cared for well and are ready for ministry.

- Well-managed financial and capital resources.

- Administration that functions as a support team that contributes to the ministry of the church.

## Chapter Nine

# DESIGNING A BUDGET
# THAT EMPOWERS THE VISION

The budget on the following pages is included here to serve as a guide. The budget must be designed to fit the major ministry areas and the ministry structures. This is very important because the budget empowers the vision. If the budget does not line up with the vision, or what the vision is seeking to work, it would not do because there would not be money allocated to that particular line item. It is essential to the vision that the budget lines up line for line, with the vision.

# Budget Sample

## WORSHIP MINISTRY

| | |
|---|---|
| Decision Makers | |
| Media Ministry | |
| Drama | |
| Usher | |
| Service Team | |
| Music | |
| Praise | |
| Ministry Support | |
| Total | |

## SHEPHERDING MINISTRY

| | |
|---|---|
| New Membership Shepherding | |
| Comfort & Care Ministry | |
| Deacon Family Care | |
| Leadership Conference & Workshop | |
| Prayer | |
| Church Development | |
| Ministry Support Staff | |
| Education: ABC Word/IOCS | |
| Total | |

## DISCIPLESHIP MINISTRY

| | |
|---|---|
| Resource Ministry | |
| New Membership | |
| Discipleship Training | |
| Home Bible Studies | |
| Life Application | |
| Adult Education | |
| Reconciliation Ministry | |
| Ministry Support Staff | |
| Total | |

# Budget Sample

## CHILDREN & YOUTH MINISTRY

| | |
|---|---|
| AWANA | |
| Children's Neighborhood Programs | |
| Children's Ministry | |
| Youth | |
| Ministry Support Staff | |
| Total | |

## EVANGELISM / MISSIONS MINISTRY

| | |
|---|---|
| Special Outreach Projects | |
| Missions | |
| Jail/Prison | |
| Transportation | |
| Evangelism | |
| Evangelism Training | |
| Ministry Support Staff | |
| Total | |

## CHRISTIAN OUTREACH CENTER

| | |
|---|---|
| Community Sponsored Programs | |
| Restoration | |
| P.A.C.E. | |
| Senior Services | |
| Political Information | |
| Outreach Residential Treatment Center | |
| Outreach Restoration Ministry | |
| Community Development Corporation | |
| Ministry Support Staff | |
| Total | |

# Budget Sample

## CHRISTIAN OUTREACH

| | |
|---|---|
| Food Pantry | |
| Clothing Pantry | |
| Probation Program | |
| Political Information Committee | |
| Outreach Restoration Ministry | |
| Community Sponsored Programs | |
| P.A.C.E. | |
| Director of Development | |
| Ministry Support Staff | |
| Total | |

## FELLOWSHIP MINISTRY

| | |
|---|---|
| Food Services | |
| Annual Event | |
| Cross Cultural Ministry | |
| Family Care Cell Fellowship | |
| Family Funship | |
| Young Adult Ministry | |
| Silver Star | |
| Sports Activities | |
| Adult Fellowships<br>• Care Cell – Men<br>• Care Cell – Women<br>• Care Cell – Singles | |
| Ministry Support Staff | |
| Total | |

# Budget Sample

## FAMILY MINISTRY

| | |
|---|---|
| Marriage | |
| Parenting | |
| Financial Planning | |
| Divorce Recovery | |
| Family Advisors | |
| Ministry Support Staff | |
| Total | |

## ADMINISTRATION

| | |
|---|---|
| Bank Chargers | |
| Copier | |
| Electric | |
| Employee Taxes | |
| Gasoline – Vans | |
| Natural Gas | |
| Insurance – Health | |
| Insurance – Flood | |
| Insurance – Property | |
| Insurance – Life | |
| Mortgage Note | |
| Janitorial Supplies | |
| Lawn Maintenance | |
| Maintenance Materials | |
| Building Equipment | |
| Equipment Repairs | |
| Maintenance Repairs | |
| Miscellaneous | |

# Budget Sample

| ADMINISTRATION (Continued) | |
|---|---|
| Office Supplies | |
| Office Equipment | |
| Petty Cash | |
| Postage | |
| Printing | |
| Professional Service | |
| Security – All Locations | |
| Security – Internal Systems | |
| Administration Support Staff | |
| Staff Training | |
| Staff Appreciation, Fringe | |
| Taxes – Other | |
| Telephone Service | |
| Trash Collection | |
| Van Maintenance | |
| Water | |
| Cell Phone | |
| Administration Cell Phones | |
| Car Lease | |
| Total | |

# Budget Sample

## FINAL TOTALS

### Ministry Areas

| | |
|---|---|
| Worship Ministry | |
| Shepherding Ministry | |
| Discipleship Ministry | |
| Children & Youth Ministry | |
| Evangelism/Ministry | |
| Christian Outreach Ministry | |
| Fellowship Ministry | |
| Family Ministry | |
| Ministries – Total | |

### Administration

| | |
|---|---|
| All Areas of Administration – Total | |

### Education

| | |
|---|---|
| Christian School Budget – Total | |

## PROPOSED  TOTAL BUDGET

_____ Church

Ministries

Administration

Education

Total (Year) Proposed  Budget

## MONTHLY BUDGET NEED

2012 Budget                    $ _____

2012 Monthly Need              $ _____

2013 Proposed Budget           $ _____

2013 Monthly Need              $ _____

Total monthly increase/decrease over last year:

$ _____

## Chapter Ten

# CONCLUSION

Developing a vision statement may seem like a tedious process and it is. It takes time to organize what the Spirit of God is doing in your ministry. It takes time to coordinate it so that the church is pointed in the direction God wants it to go. The most important component in this process is to conduct every plan, every activity, from a biblical perspective grounded in the will of God. That is the way to ensure that your church is empowered by the Spirit of God. The members are strengthened, the path and direction for sermons and Bible study is set, and the pastor is at peace because he is at the center of God's will and can have confidence that God will grant success to the ministry.

Every place on which the sole of your foot treads, I have given it to you, just as I spoke to Moses. From the wilderness and this Lebanon, even as far the great river, the river Euphrates, all the land of the Hittites, and as far as the Great Sea toward the setting of the sun will be your territory. No man will be able to stand before you all the days of your life. Just as I have been with Moses, I will be with you; I will not fail you or forsake you. Be strong and courageous, for you shall give this people possession of the land which I swore to their fathers to give them. Only be strong and very courageous; be careful to do according to all the law which Moses My servant commanded you; do not turn from it to the right or to the left, so that you may have success wherever you go. This book of law shall not depart from your mouth, but you shall meditate on it day and night, so that you may be careful to do according to all that is written in it for them you will make your prosperous, and then you will have success. Have I not commanded you? Be strong and courageous! Do not tremble or be dismayed, for the Lord your God is with you wherever you go (Joshua 1:3–9).

I strongly urge pastors to let the ministry areas drive the sermon and Bible study planning. He can do a series on each area, e.g. orderly functioning ("do all things decently and in order"); giving, leadership, building the church. Before a pastor develops a series, he may want to do a couple of sermons about the church's change of direction.

The Sunday school curriculum can be revised to challenge people to become involved in the new strategy of the church.

## CONSIDER RETREATING

The pastor might want to consider a long retreat with associate pastors, staff, some of the elders or the "Peter, James, and John" deacons (the deacons that show the greatest spirituality or the most supportive deacons). Include existing ministry leaders, and those that have been recruited to the coordinator positions. Include people that may be supportive, but not yet involved.

1.  To start the retreat, spend time explaining the biblical nature of the vision. Show how the Bible supports the vision so that all leaders understand that it is God's vision. Spend time explaining the ministry outlines. Seek to create as much discussion as possible and allow the associate pastors to become involved. Once each ministry outline has been explained, show how each ministry outline ties into the vision and the ministry structures.

2.  Break them into small groups with the associate pastors leading each ministry area so anyone can ask questions and be reassured that everything is working for the glory of God. Then spend the last part of the retreat explaining the budgetary implications of the new plan. Make sure everyone has a clear understanding, and that they leave the retreat excited and committed to work cohesively to implement the vision. Spend time throughout the retreat praying for God to have His way.

3. After the retreat, call a church business meeting so that the new strategy can be exposed to the church. Notice that this is not done until elders, deacons, associate pastors, ministers, ministry leaders and supporters are fully informed and largely supportive of the vision. This is important because if anyone in the body rises up to attack the vision after the meeting, there should be several people who can defend it intelligently or answer their questions informatively. This creates a greater level of confidence in the congregation about the vision. It also generates support because of the level of respect the pastor has provided to the members and other leaders. Instead of seeing a pastor who demands that they do what God has laid on his heart, members will see a pastor who has expressed what God wants done and has given them time to absorb and become a viable participant in the process. Throughout this entire process, get together with some pastor friends or some of the elders or deacons and spend time praying that God blesses the process and implementation of the vision. Always seek to present it as the Lord's vision that He has laid on your heart to implement. Do not present it as your vision that God wants you to do.

4. After all this has been done, revisit the vision and its process with all the leaders to make sure that they remain clear and supportive. Meet with each associate pastor regularly and collectively at least once a month.

Nehemiah was a man of God with a clear vision from God, and he had the support of God and his king. He still had to convince the people, deal with enemies and do the work of rebuilding the walls. Because of his dedication to the process, his passion to see it through, his sacrifice in being an active part of this plan, and his willingness to work like everyone else, his leadership was contagious and it blessed God's kingdom.

Let these scriptures shape the life of your ministry:

Let love be without hypocrisy. Abhor what is evil; cling to what is good. Be devoted to one another in brotherly love; give preference to one another in honor; not lagging behind in diligence, fervent in spirit, serving the Lord; rejoicing in hope, preserving in tribulation, devoted to prayer, contributing to the needs of the saints, practicing hospitality. Bless those who persecute you; bless and do not curse. Rejoice with those who rejoice, and weep with those who weep. Be of the same mind toward one another; do not be haughty in mind, but associate with the lowly. Do not be wise in your own estimation. Never pay back evil for evil to anyone. Respect what is right in the sight of all men. If possible, so far as it depends on you, be at peace with all men (Rom. 12:3–21).

Therefore my beloved brethren, be steadfast, immovable, always abounding in the work of the Lord, knowing that your toil is not in vain in the Lord (1 Cor. 15:58).

# Appendix

# MINISTRY FLOW CHARTS

Sheep & Ministry Development

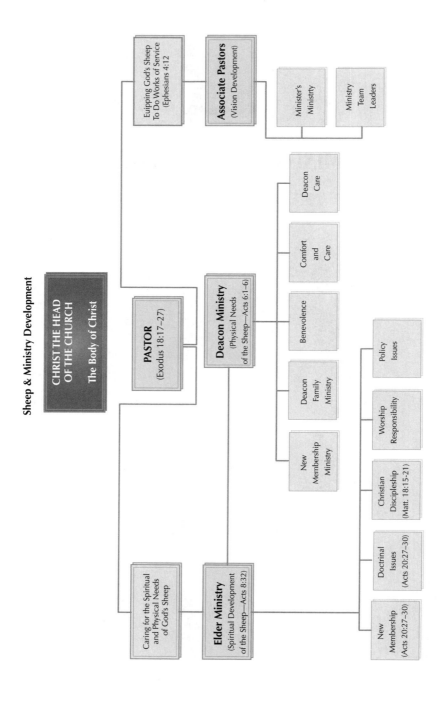

# Deacon Ministry

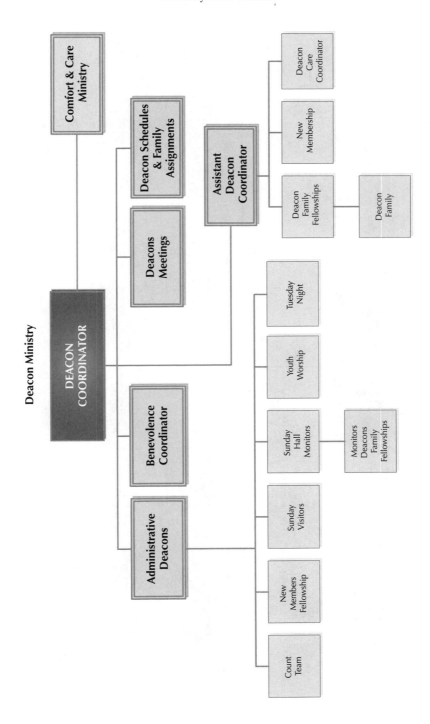

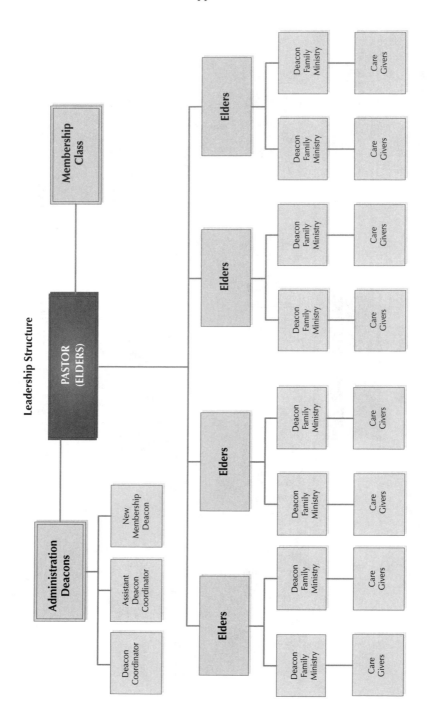

Leadership Structure

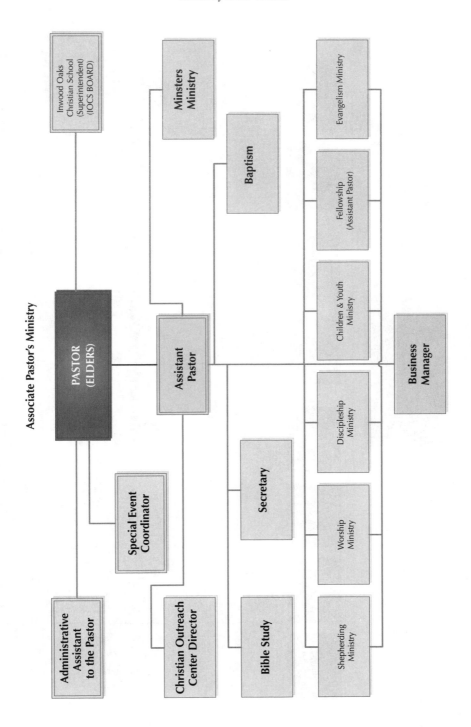

Associate Pastor's Ministry

Inwood Oaks Christian School (Superintendent) (IOCS BOARD)

PASTOR (ELDERS)

Administrative Assistant to the Pastor

Special Event Coordinator

Christian Outreach Center Director

Minsters Ministry

Baptism

Assistant Pastor

Secretary

Bible Study

Evangelism Ministry

Fellowship (Assistant Pastor)

Children & Youth Ministry

Discipleship Ministry

Worship Ministry

Shepherding Ministry

Business Manager

# Appendix

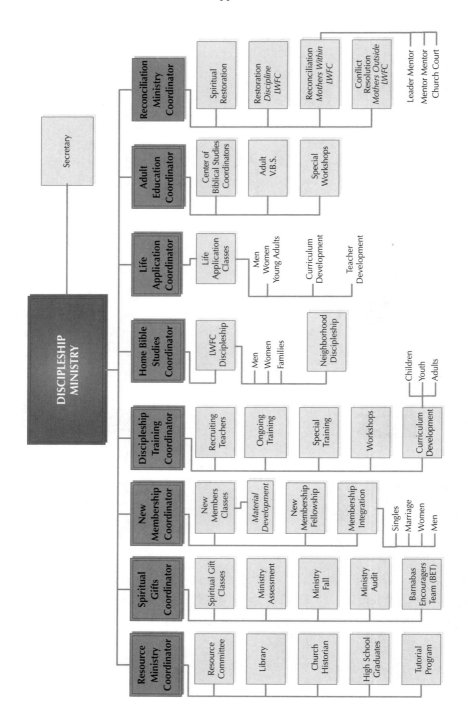

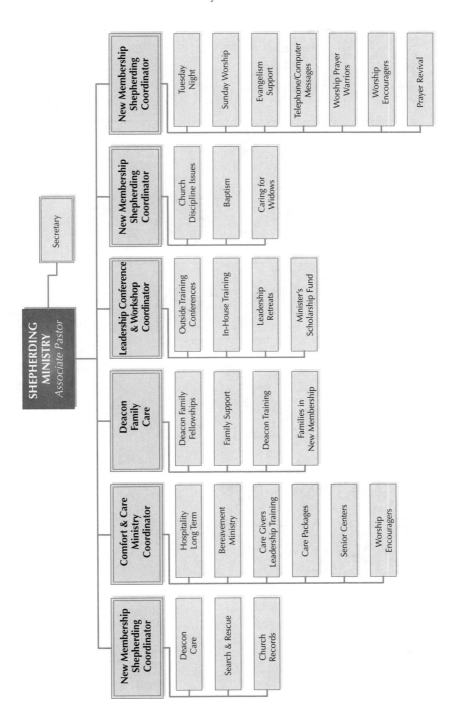

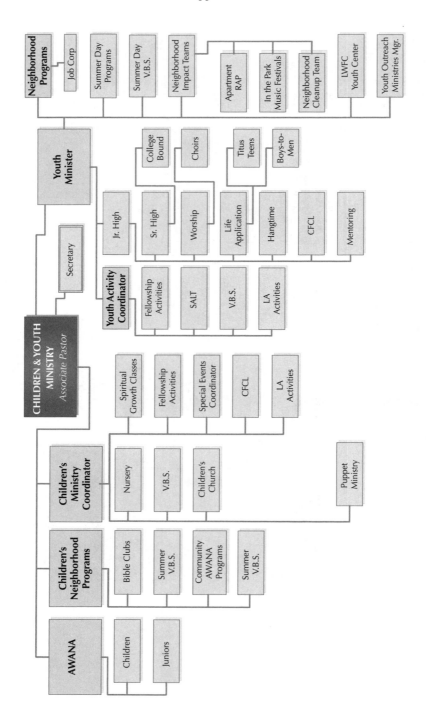

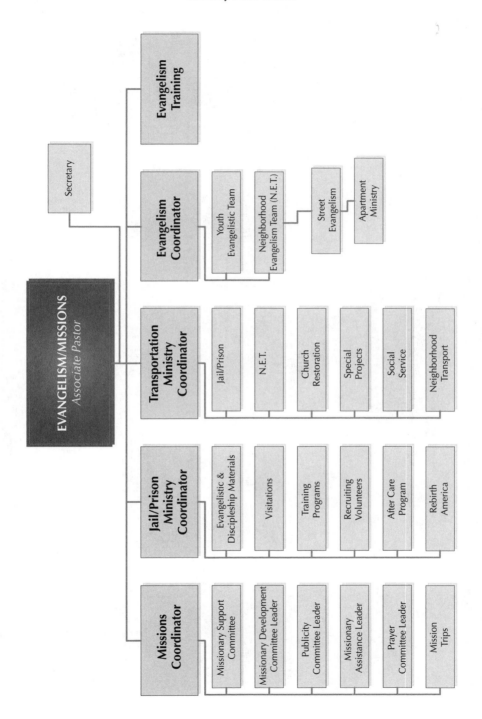

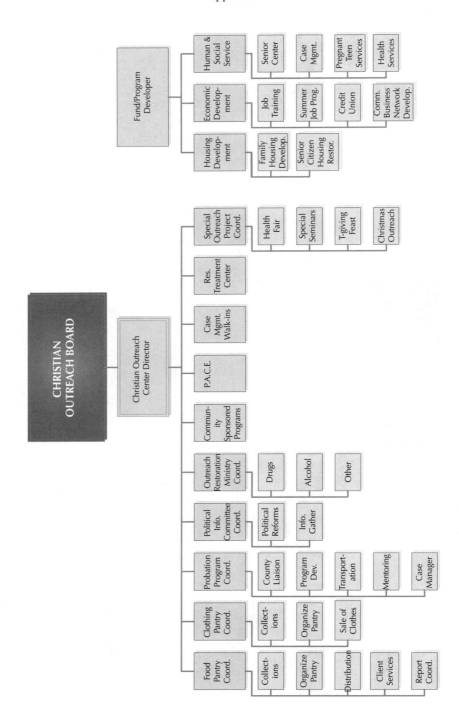

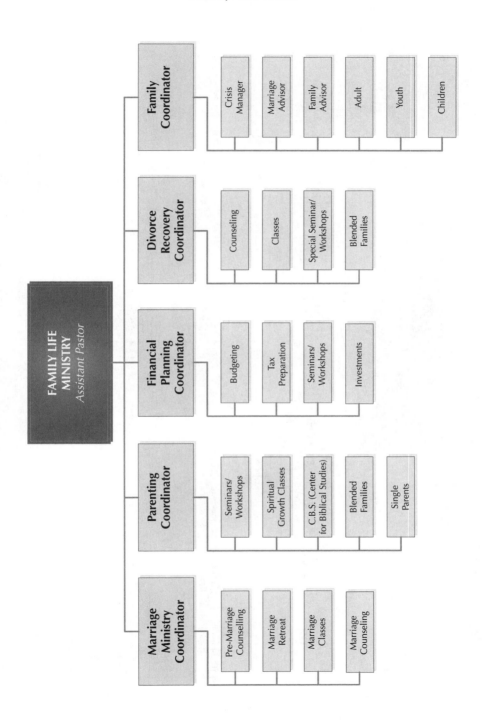

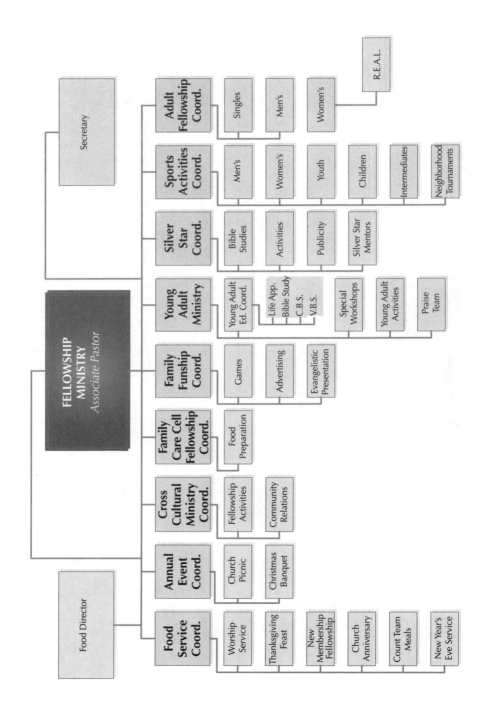